TR

Francis Fergusson

Trope and Allegory

Themes Common to
Dante and Shakespeare

Athens
The University of Georgia Press

Library of Congress Catalog Card Number: 76–12684
International Standard Book Number: 0–8203–0410–7

The University of Georgia Press, Athens 30602

Set in 12 on 14 point Linotype Garamond No. 3
Printed in the United States of America

Contents

Acknowledgments

Much of the material in this book has appeared before in different form, and I wish to thank those persons who have permitted me to use it here: *Dante Studies*, 1968; the Gauss Seminars, Princeton University; the *Sewanee Review*, 1975.

TROPE AND ALLEGORY

I

The Common Heritage
of Dante and Shakespeare

There is no reason to think that Shakespeare ever read
Dante, but in recent years the kinship between them, based
on their medieval heritage, has come to be recognized in
various ways. Pound and Eliot, when they were doing their
reading fifty or sixty years ago, both felt it. Perhaps that
was because they came from this side of the Atlantic, and
so brought to the study of European literature a new ob-
jectivity, a fresh freedom from the reigning prejudices.
Since then a number of important scholars have studied
aspects of Shakespeare's medieval heritage. In this book I
have made as much use as I could of E. M. W. Tillyard's
writings, especially his *Shakespeare's History Plays*,[1] and
also of Erich Auerbach's, especially his *Mimesis* and his
Figura.[2]

There are plenty of differences between Dante and
Shakespeare, some of which will be brought out in what
follows. But it is clear to anyone who reads them carefully
that they share that classical-Christian vision of human nature and destiny which was composed of Aristotelian philosophy, Christian theology, and the heritage of pagan and
biblical literature made relevant to their time by allegorical interpretation. That of course was the accepted "world

picture," as Tillyard called it; and it was available to any poet of the time. But so far as I know only Dante at the beginning of the Renaissance and Shakespeare at the end were able to use it in all its harmonious complexity to mirror earthly life. Perhaps that is what Eliot had in mind when he portentously remarked, "Shakespeare and Dante divide the modern world between them; there is no third."[3]

Their immediate aims as poets were of course quite different. Dante was writing in the *Commedia* the unified epic of his own journey of enlightenment, while Shakespeare in the course of his twenty-eight years of playwrighting was presenting a great variety of versions of human comedy and tragedy. Nevertheless their conceptions of the art and the purpose of poetry were similar. When Hamlet tells the players that the purpose of their art is "to hold, as 'twere, the mirror up to nature; to show virtue her own feature, scorn her own image, and the very age and body of the time his form and pressure,"[4] and Dante tells Can Grande that his aim in the *Commedia* was to show "man, as by good or ill deserts, in the exercise of the freedom of his choice, he becomes liable to punishing or rewarding justice,"[5] they are in essential agreement. Dante adopts the make-believe of the postmortem journey, while Shakespeare always creates an earthly setting, but both wished to imitate human action as we learn to recognize it on earth, and to reveal its God-given meaning.

That is partly because they were both brought up on that Aristotelian ethics, metaphysics, and psychology which was the standard philosophy from Dante's Aquinas to Shakespeare's Hooker. In the *Poetics* Aristotle writes: "Life consists in action, and its end [or aim] is a mode of action";[6]

action is at the base of his philosophy of man. When Hamlet speaks of mirroring nature and when Dante names "man . . . in the exercise of the freedom of his choice," they both assume Aristotle's view. And they both (though they did not know the *Poetics*) have the Aristotelian idea that poetry is the imitation of action. They knew that they wanted to represent human nature, which they had learned to understand as Aristotle did.

Both poets are responsible for the meanings of the actions they imitate, as the quotations from *Hamlet* and from the letter to Can Grande show. Dante is quite clear about the meanings he built into the *Commedia:* in his Letter 10 to Can Grande he associates them with the four meanings traditionally found in biblical narrative: Letter, Allegory, Trope (or moral meaning), and anagoge. He explains:

> And this mode of treatment, for its better manifestation, may be considered in this verse: "When Israel came out of Egypt, and the house of Jacob from a people of strange speech, Judas became his sanctification, Israel his power." For if we inspect the letter alone, the departure of the children of Israel from Egypt in the time of Moses is presented to us; if the allegory, our redemption wrought by Christ; if the moral sense, the conversion of the soul from the grief and misery of sin to the state of grace is presented to us; if the anagogical, the departure of the holy soul from the slavery of this corruption to the liberty of eternal glory is presented to us. And although these mystic senses have each their special denominations, they may all in general be called allegorical, since they differ from the literal and historical. (Letter 10, par. 7)

The three meanings of the Letter, which gives the literal action, may be thought of as dimensions of that action. The

Allegory defines it with reference to the faith that moves it, ultimately in this tradition, faith in Christ. The moral meaning is focused on the moving or turning psyche itself, and the Anagoge signifies the ultimate, unseen goal of all human action: God. When Dante in his *De Monarchia* (book 3:xvi) discussed the two goals of action here on earth, "the blessedness of this life" and "the blessedness of eternal life," he was thinking of action with a moral meaning and then of action moved by faith: "For to the first we attain by the teachings of philosophy, following them by acting in accordance with the moral and intellectual virtues: To the second by spiritual teachings which transcend human reason, as we follow them by acting according to the theological virtues: faith, hope, to wit, and charity."[7] And when he composed the *Commedia* he staged himself as he made the fictive trip getting only the letter, the literal action, in Hell, without either moral or religious understanding; then as he climbed the Mount of Purgatory with Virgil learning to get the moral meaning of the journey, and when he met his beloved Beatrice at the top of the mountain seeing the allegory: the beautiful but incomprehensible process of Revelation centered in Christ. The anagoge he saves for the *Paradiso*, which is devoted to *La gloria di Colui che tutto move*, ("The glory of Him who moves all things").[8]

Shakespeare does not always employ the traditional allegory (as he did in *The Merchant of Venice*, labelling its elements), but he saw the meanings of his plays as moral and religious, and sometimes points that out. Hamlet's definition of the purpose of the theater art, for example, refers to the letter, the trope, and the allegory. "Holding the mirror up to nature," describes the letter; "showing virtue her own feature, scorn her own image," indicates the moral meaning; and "the age and body of the time, his form and pressure," refers to the allegory, the meaning of the historic moment which can be had in Shakespeare's tradition only by faith in Christ. Shakespeare does not mention the anagoge, for like Dante in *De Monarchia*, the *Inferno*, and the *Purgatorio* he treats only earthly life and not the mystic vision of heaven; but he sees the meaning of earthly life very much as Dante does.

In considering the allegory of Dante or Shakespeare it is essential to remember that it is far more realistic than the allegory we are more familiar with. The three meanings are thought of as *contained* in the letter, as Dante and his masters frequently remind us. In Dante's example the actual journey of the Hebrews to the promised land comes first, with all its dust and noise and fatigue and terror, and only by realizing that can we get its moral, religious, or mystic meanings. This feature was plain to the exegetes from before Dante to Shakespeare. Thomas Aquinas put it this way: "In Holy Writ no confusion results, for all the interpretations are founded on one, the literal."[9] William Whitaker, an Anglican divine contemporary with Shakespeare, is in agreement: "We concede such things as allegory, anagoge and tropology in Scripture," he writes, "but meanwhile we deny that there are many and various senses. We affirm that there is but one true, proper and genuine sense of Scripture, arising from the words rightly understood, which we call the literal: and we contend that allegories, tropologies and anagoges are not various senses, but various collections from one sense, or various applications and accommodations of that one meaning."[10] Shakespeare writes in that tradition: he gives us his story as real, but as having the moral and religious meanings that make it significant.

Shakespeare's realism distinguishes him from most of his contemporaries and assimilates him to Dante and to certain medieval doctrines. Auerbach in his *Mimesis* studied this medieval realism, the basis of the fourfold allegory of Dante; and he enabled us to distinguish it sharply from the kind that C. S. Lewis studied in his *Allegory of Love*,[11] which is more familiar to readers of English than the full medieval variety. Lewis's allegory is essentially a matter of personifying such abstract concepts as Peace, War, the Virtues, the Vices. Lewis finds it in Bunyan, the *Roman de la Rose*, Spenser, and many other places. He excludes Dante from his "allegory of love" explicitly, and Shakespeare by simple omission. In that he is right, for though Dante and Shakespeare can use personification when they need it—as well as icons, liturgical symbols, pagan gods—their allegory rises essentially out of the dramatic interplay of "real" people. Their fictions are intended to reflect not our concepts but the actual world, in which God's own meaning was supposed to be embodied (if we could only learn to see it) just as it was supposed to be in the events recorded in Scripture.

In what follows I shall try to bring out the literal meaning of my examples first, and then the meanings the authors wished it to show.

II

Romantic Love as Lost

Paolo and Francesca
and Romeo and Juliet

By romantic love I mean that cult which began with the
Provençal poets and continued, in many changing versions,
through Shakespeare's time. Ezra Pound studied it in "The
Spirit of Romance,"[1] and many other authors have dealt
with various aspects of it. It was a common theme in renaissance literature, and it is of course of crucial importance in
Dante's work from Beatrice's appearance in the *Vita Nuova*
to the *Paradiso* at the end of his career. It is the theme of all
of Shakespeare's romantic comedies, and he returns to it in
his four last plays, especially *The Winter's Tale* and *The
Tempest*.

In the *Purgatorio* Dante presents his romantic love for
Beatrice—or rather the faith in her which it inspires—as
ultimately the chief clue to the motivation of that poem.
Until he reaches the *Paradiso Terrestre* at the top of the
mountain Dante is following Virgil, who represents the
right rule which had been attained by the pagan world;
but we are reminded all along that it was Beatrice who
caused Virgil to guide Dante, and when she finally appears
she completely replaces Virgil with her different illumina-

tion. One may say that the *Purgatorio* is a story of two motivations: the rational attempt to follow Virgil's right rule
and the extrarational attachment to Beatrice. Both are
needed by the Pilgrim. Shakespeare in his second period,
when he wrote only his greatest history plays, *Romeo and
Juliet*, and his romantic comedies, was exploring the same
two motivations—one based on faith in the right rule of the
right king, the other on faith in the beloved woman. In
Shakespeare faith in the monarchy is more seriously handled
than romantic love. He does not explore the ultimate postmortem meanings of romance as Dante does; he meets it
only in the real world, and usually in youth, where it is
bound to be dreamy, comic, and fragmentary. Nevertheless
he sees the phenomenon itself—the ur-passion of romantic
love—very much as Dante does.

Romance was a common theme in literature from the
time of Dante to that of Shakespeare, but they knew more
about it than anyone else. They present it with such immediate poetic power that their readers, including many of
their critics, are seduced; but neither of them was seduced:
they were able to realize the experience to the full and at
the same time see it in the wider context of their whole
view of man's life. I don't propose to try to define romance,
but instead to describe the vision of it which Dante and
Shakespeare share. They find in it three traits, which one
can discover in all their pictures of it.

First of all, romantic love is confined to those that Dante
calls the *gentili*, the "gentle" or "noble." Guinizelli, the
father of Dante's school, the *stil novisti*, proclaimed that
"love and the gentle heart are one thing"; and the poets of
this school, especially Dante, often repeated that basic ar-

ticle of their esoteric creed. In the *Convivio*[2] Dante explains what he means by *gentilezza:* it is a gift of God, a quality of spirit which manifests itself in different ways at different times of life. As an unearned and unpredictable gift, like physical grace and beauty, it has nothing to do with the virtues, though with proper training it may be made the basis of virtue. It also has nothing to do with gentleness of birth or with any kind of inherited wealth or social position. In the *Convivio* Dante's account of *gentilezza* is part of his vigorous polemic against the snobbery of wealth or status. Shakespeare seems to have a more snobbish view of this trait, for in his plays the gentle are almost invariably of gentle birth. In other respects, however, his romantic lovers conform to Dante's formula. They didn't earn their beauty of mind or spirit, and much of their experience is not measurable by rational moral standards. He invariably contrasts his gentle, privileged romantic lovers with earthier comic types, and this formula—the polite melodious lovers ironically accompanied by a more cheerful and bawdy pair, usually servants—lasts in European comedy at least to the end of the eighteenth century.

The second trait of romantic love is that it demands total commitment and obedience. The stern warning which Bassanio finds on the leaden casket that contains Portia's picture—that he must "give and hazard all he hath"—applies to all true lovers in this tradition. It is no doubt connected with the rules of *amor cortese,* the feudal obedience the lover owes to his *donna;* but Dante and Shakespeare always show the natural psychological basis of that convention, and so make it significant to us now. Only the *gentili* are capable of devoting *all* their love to one object, and so get

completely carried away: their more pedestrian counter-
parts love food and money too, and therefore can more
easily keep their feet on the ground.

The third trait of total love of this kind is that when it
first appears it always strikes its victim as a mystery. I quote
the first sonnet in the *Vita Nuova,* which Dante says he
wrote for the other "lieges of love" to beg them to help him
interpret the love which had just come to him:

> To every captive soul and gentle heart, into whose presence
>   come the present rhymes, that they may write me back
>   their opinion—Greeting in their lord, to wit, Love.
> Already nigh a third of the hours of the time that every
> star is
>   bright to us, had passed, when suddenly Love appeared
>   to me, the memory of whose being maketh me shudder.
> Gladsome Love seemed to me, holding my heart in his hand,
>   and in his arms he had my lady, wrapped in a drapery and
>   sleeping.
> Then he awakened her and of this flaming heart, she fearful,
>   did humbly eat: afterwards I beheld him go his way a-
>   weeping.[3]

This little poem has the ambiguity and ambivalence and
tension which we have been taught to prize in modern lyrics—and no wonder, for like many modern works it is intended to imitate a *moto spiritale* at the most immediate and
intimate point: before the sufferer knows at all what to
make of it.

Such is the basic passion of romantic love. Dante and
Shakespeare are both careful to show how dangerous it is if
obeyed literally, before one takes time to investigate its

meanings; and also how life-giving it may be for those who hang onto it as it changes its appearance and slowly leads on to deeper understanding. Dante showed it as lost, in the Paolo-Francesca episode in *Inferno* 5; and Shakespeare showed it that way in *Romeo and Juliet*.

Anyone who reads *Inferno* 5 (the canto which recounts the story of Paolo and Francesca) and *Romeo and Juliet* must feel that the two works present very similar visions of youthful love when it leads to death. This love is in both cases strictly romantic: a passion of the *gentili* which demands total commitment, mysterious though it is to the lovers. In both cases it is obeyed literally, before its meanings can be realized, and that is one sufficient reason why it leads to death. Shakespeare presents it in a populous full-length play, Dante in a few lines in one canto; and their methods are therefore necessarily different. But at the same time the principles of their plot-making, their characterization, and their symbolism or metaphorical structure are closely analogous, for both poets are imitating the same action: literal obedience to romantic love.

By the time we reach Paolo and Francesca in canto 5 their story has been prepared for in various ways. We know from the laconic inscription on Hell Gate in canto 3 that Primal Love makes all hell: "fecemi . . . il primo Amore." We glimpsed the process when we saw the lost souls gathering on the bank of Acheron and then being wafted across like falling leaves in autumn. We were told that when they reach that shore, *la tema si volge in disio*—"fear is turned into desire." These movements of spirit and these modes of awareness soften us up, so to say, make us ready to respond to Paolo and Francesca almost as swiftly as they respond to each other.

In canto 5, as soon as we meet the dames and cavaliers of old blown on their dark wind, we feel the tyrannous atmosphere of their romantic love; and Francesca, when we meet her, uses the melodious language of *amor cortese*. As she starts her story she might be beginning a love song in the *dolce stil nuovo*, and her first line refers to what I have called the basic creed of the *fedeli d'amore: amor, ch'a cor gentil ratto s'apprende* ("love, which in gentle heart is quickly caught"). The first line of her second tercet is a singularly suggestive version of the total commitment her love demands: *Amor, ch'a nullo amato amar perdona* ("love, which excuses no one who is loved from loving," as it may be clumsily translated). As for the third crucial trait, the mysteriousness of love when it first strikes, Francesca does not mention it, presumably because it never occurred to her to question what so powerfully moved her. But the line which begins the third tercet, abruptly truncating the love song—*amor condusse noi ad una morte* ("love led us to one death")—must leave one with a most painful sense of the incomprehensibility of her experience.

Shakespeare, like Dante, relies on a sonnet, which his chorus uses to open *Romeo and Juliet*, to orient us toward his romantic theme—"the fearful passage of their death-marked love." But he must, in scene 1, introduce the town of Verona where the story, which he took from Bandello,[4] occurs. Bandello's version is a charming tale of love, but Shakespeare transforms it, lifting it to the level of poetry by seeing its love as ancient romance, and seeing romance where it belongs in the traditional classical-Christian philosophy. Here in scene 1 he presents Romeo's love as one of the passions which the young in Verona must suffer in the dog days. So he establishes the action of the play as a whole: "to handle the reckless young passions of summer," for we see that the prince, the friar, the lovers' parents must all try to control both Romeo's love and the hatred of Tybalt. So Romeo's romance is "placed" by analogy with the other passions of youth.

The first scene presents the basic situation in Verona. On a hot street the animal spirits of the young, pugnacious or erotic, are ready to explode; and the partisans of the Capulets get into a pointless but pleasurable brawl with the partisans of the Montagues. Old Montague and old Capulet are soon involved; then the prince arrives, threatens those who were responsible, and dismisses the fighters. Their departure is soon followed by the moping entrance of Romeo, who, we learn, is a "captive soul" already, for love had seized him when he looked at the unwilling Rosaline. He explains his condition, which he sees as closely analogous to that of the fighters:

> Alas that love, whose view is muffled still,
> Should without eyes see pathways to his will.
> Where shall we dine? O me, what fray was here?
> Yet tell me not, for I have heard it all.
> Here's much to do with hate, but more with love.
> Why then, O brawling love, O loving hate,
> O any thing of nothing first create!
> O heavy lightness, serious vanity,
> Misshapen chaos of well-seeming forms,

> Feather of lead, bright smoke, cold fire, sick health,
> Still-waking sleep that is not what it is!
> This love I feel, that feel no love in this.　　　　(1.1)

Romeo is describing the same bewildering experience, with its incomprehensible promises of all or nothing, that the young Dante speaks of in the sonnet that I quoted. In a sense he "knows" his condition very well, but his knowledge is of a kind that can do him no good. Aristotle (in *Nicomachean Ethics* 7.3)[5] points out that we may often know something in a way that does not avail to guide us, and this commonplace of his psychology is important in both Dante and Shakespeare. Shakespeare's tragic characters often see their erring motives clearly, even as they obey them; and Dante in hell often "knows" with his head without being able to save himself from sharing the experience, and even the motivation, of the damned.

In the next three scenes of act 1 most of the characters are sketched, and the Capulet party is set up. Romeo, a Montague, is of course not invited, but he and his friends resolve to go anyway. These scenes are filled with the riches of Shakespeare's young imagination, the whole restless scene in summertime Verona: the kind of playful elaboration characteristic of Shakespeare and quite foreign to Dante. But it all leads to the party, and there both forms of passion find their fated foci. Romeo meets Juliet:

> O she doth teach the torches to burn bright.
> It seems she hangs upon the cheek of night
> As a rich jewel in an Ethiop's ear.　　　　(1.5)

At the same time Tybalt spots Romeo and tells Capulet he'll not endure the hated Montague. When Capulet restrains

him, he growls, "Patience perforce with wilful choler meeting / Makes my flesh tremble in their different greeting,"
and departs in fury. We then hear at once the delicate greeting which Romeo (whose flesh trembles for a different
reason) offers his Juliet:

> If I profane with my unworthiest hand
> This holy shrine, the gentle sin is this,
> My lips two blushing pilgrims ready stand
> To smooth that rough touch with a tender kiss.

The two find their way through the sonnets they exchange
to a kiss, when the nurse interrupts. The party is over, Romeo and Juliet must part, but they know their sudden love is
destined to have its way with them.

The first act is of course quite different from the sequence
in the *Commedia* that leads to Paolo and Francesca, but it
serves to introduce the same fatal passion. The rest of the
play is also many times as long as Dante's brief episode, but
it is handled analogously, as one may see by comparing the
plots, the characterization, and the symbolism of the two
works.

I have already mentioned the fact that both poets choose
characters who are not only *gentili* but young; the young
are the most capable of "hazarding all," and the least able
to wait patiently until their love reveals its meanings. When
he first sees Paolo and Francesca, Dante separates them from
the older victims of lust: "Poet, willingly would I speak
with those two that go together and seem so light upon the
wind." He then plots the narrative in order to give the impression of great speed. This is partly achieved by recount-
ing his relation to Francesca at the same time she tells us
of hers to Paolo. Dante, as he listens, is overcome almost

at once, and we see that Francesca from the first could not resist Paolo. Francesca's final narrative, in answer to Dante's question how love permitted them "to know the dubious desires," is only twenty-one lines long, but every bit of it embodies that movement of spirit which consists in being moved, immediately and irresistibly. The two swift sequences end when Francesca says, "*quel glorno più non vi leggemmo avanti*" ("that day we read in it no further"), and Dante faints with pity.

Shakespeare also took care to make his plot give the effect of speed. The action is all concentrated between Sunday and Thursday night, and it is like a race between Romeo and Juliet and Tybalt, and between the young and the older Veronese. While Romeo is meeting Juliet, marrying her, and spending his one night with her, Tybalt kills Mercutio and Romeo kills Tybalt, thereby incurring his banishment to Padua. The racing effect is repeated when Juliet's funeral overtakes her wedding to Paris, and again when Romeo, Paris, and the friar all rush to Juliet's tomb at the end of the play. Both poets use the plot to show how their lovers lacked the time to learn anything about the love they were so desperately obeying.

Dante's imagery is of course much simpler than Shakespeare's. It begins with the dark wind on which the lovers ride, and it continues with the three images of birds borne on their wings (or their desires) and with the River Po descending to its rest in the sea. These movements are all passive, and they represent what love did to Paolo and Francesca: caught Paolo, caught Francesca, and carried them to one death. The tonality of romance is maintained by Francesca's broken sonnet, which reminds one of what Dante

himself had written in the *Vita Nuova;* by Lancelot, the
great hero of romance whose capture by love completes
Paolo's and Francesca's capture as they read *per diletto;* and
above all by Francesca's wonderfully simple language which
gives us directly her total obedience to love.

In Shakespeare's play also the imagery establishes the
atmosphere of romance, which is literally suggested by the
sonnets of the chorus and the lovers. Shakespeare stages the
lovers' night together, and the dawn which follows it, like
a Provençal *aubade.* The imagery of night versus daylight,
which is in the whole play, is derived from romance: daylight separates the lovers, night brings them together.
When Romeo sees Juliet at the party she appears like a rich
jewel in an Ethiop's ear; the dark apothecary from whom
Romeo purchases his death contrasts with the friar, whose
wisdom brings light. The wedding that turns into a funeral
is a plot device mirroring the course of this love into darkness, much as the wedding-funeral confusion in *Much Ado
About Nothing* mirrors a love moving the other way,
toward life and light. Dante has room only for the dark air
on which his lovers ride, but Shakespeare can present the
love "whose view is muffled still," the love that without eyes
can see "pathways to his will," with a rich interplay of light
and dark throughout the play. Thus the imageries of the
two poets are differently developed, but they are similar in
principle, for they imitate the same vision of romantic love.

One may be tempted to see the "death-marked" love of
Paolo and Francesca and of Romeo and Juliet as the love
of death. Denis de Rougemont has traced the love of death
in the romantic tradition from the Provençal poets to its
culmination in Wagner's *Tristan und Isolde.*[6] He shows

how Wagner makes his romantic love into a mystique signifying infinitely desirable death. This passion is the one reality here on earth; in the Tristan story, as Wagner tells it, it determines not only the characters but the whole world in which they exist, pointing always to the mystic void of death. But Dante and Shakespeare do not see passion as the one reality; they see it as one condition suffered by their young people, and their young people as inhabiting a world created not by passion but by God. Paolo and Francesca and Romeo and Juliet may often see their world as passion paints it for them—and so may the reader. But Dante and Shakespeare do not: they see the world, with their "medieval realism," as real; and their lovers' passion as only one mode of human love. And they are both careful to indicate where it fits in the scale of human loves, even as they seduce their readers with it.

Dante of course places the love of Paolo and Francesca in the huge context of the whole *Commedia;* but when we first meet it, in hell where "the good of the intellect is lost," he makes it feel to us, as it does to them, like the sole reality. Dante is told by Virgil that Paolo and Francesca sinned through lust, but that bit of knowledge does not reach him intimately enough to render him immune: he *actually* knows only their literal state, and he can beg Francesca "by the love that leads them" to explain that love to him. Francesca, who feels the love in Dante's voice, obeys. The language of love is the only means of communication in this circle, and by sticking to it Dante gives the reader only a literal—and therefore irresistible—knowledge; and the proper end of the sequence is Dante's fainting.

One must think over the Paolo and Francesca episode

when one recovers from it, if one is to see where it fits in the great scheme. Where we encounter it at the beginning of Hell proper, it serves as an "easy descent into Avernus" by dramatizing Dante's own lost movement of spirit. It points all the way down to the bottom of Hell, where we meet Ugolino and Ruggieri. Their treachery having cut the root of their love now ties them together in hatred, to all eternity; and their confinement in hatred is analogous to Paolo's and Francesca's confinement in the passion of love. When Dante at last emerges from Hell and slowly explores Purgatory, he meets a carefully ordered series of female figures, each of which reveals the love that moves him then. The climax of the purgatorial sequence is in his meeting with Beatrice at the top of the mountain. It is, however, Piccarda di Donati, whom Dante meets in the moon (canto 3), the beginning of the *Paradiso*, who most clearly "places" Francesca. Piccarda is, like Francesca, a simple woman simply moved by love; but while Francesca is moved by her total passion for Paolo, Piccarda is moved by charity, the love of God. Francesca inhabits the bank of the Po as that river descends to its rest in the sea, moving in obedience to gravity; but Piccarda moves only in obedience to the Divine will, which is *quel mare al qual tutto si move* ("that sea to which all moves"). Just as Francesca embodies Dante's action as he yields, and enters hell, so Piccarda embodies it as he enters *Paradiso*, opening and freeing his love to apprehend the whole "sea of Being." Francesca's love is determined by its object: Paolo as he literally appears. Piccarda's is determined by *its* object: God, Being itself, the source of all meaning.

The scene of Shakespeare's play is the earthly human

town of Verona, where Romeo's love is as hard to place as it
would be in any town. But the friar sees that human world
within the whole cosmos, and Shakespeare uses him to place
Romeo's and Juliet's relentless infatuation where it belongs in God's universe. We first meet the friar early in the
morning after the Capulet party, collecting herbs in his
garden, and rejoicing in the wonderful and perilous order
of the natural world:

> The earth that's nature's mother is her tomb;
> What is her burying grave that is her womb.
> And from her womb children of divers kind
> We sucking on her natural bosom find;
> Many for many virtues excellent;
> None but for some, and yet all different.
> O mickle is the powerful grace that lies
> In plants, herbs, stones, and their true qualities.
> For naught so vile that on the earth doth live,
> But to the earth some special good doth give;
> For naught so good, but strained from that fair use,
> Revolts from true birth, stumbling on abuse.
>
> .   .   .   .
>
> Two such opposed kings encamp them still
> In man as well as herbs—grace and rude will;
> And where the worser is predominant,
> Full soon the canker death eats up that plant.   (2.3)

The friar's vision is like Virgil's, as he explains it in *Purgatorio* 17 and 18: the love that moves all creatures, an-
imate and inanimate, plant, animal, and human, may produce either good or evil, depending on the "use" made of
it. Or it might be described as a humble version of what
Beatrice tells Dante in *Paradiso* 1 as they miraculously ride
to the stars:

e cominciò: "Le cose tutte quante
    hanno ordine tra loro, e questo è forma
    che l'universo a Dio fa simigliante.

  .   .   .   .

Ne l'ordine ch'io dico sono accline
    tutte nature, per diverse sorti,
    più al principio loro e men vicine;
onde si muovono a diversi porti
    per lo gran mar de l'essere, . . .

  .   .   .   .

Vero è che, come forma non s'accorda
    molte fïate a l'intenzion de l'arte,
    perch' a risponder la materia è sorda
cosi da questo corso si diparte
    talor la creatura.   (1.103–131 passim)

(And she began: All things whatsoever have order among
themselves, and this is the form that makes the universe
resemble God. . . . In the order I speak of all natures have
their bent according to their different lots, nearer to their
source and farther from it; they move, therefore, to different ports over the great sea of being, each with an
instinct given it to bear it on. . . . It is true that, as a shape
often does not accord with the art's intention because the
material is deaf and unresponsive, so sometimes the creature, having the power, thus impelled, to turn aside
another way, deviates from this course.)

Infatuated Romeo appears toward the end of the friar's discourse, and we are ready to see his love deviating from the
divine order. The friar at once tries to explain this to him:

Is Rosaline, that thou didst love so dear,
So soon forsaken? Young men's love then lies
Not truly in their hearts but in their eyes.   (2.3)

And when Romeo tells him that Rosaline did not, like Juliet, "grace for grace and love for love allow," the friar answers: "O, she knew well / Thy love did read by rote that could not spell." He means that Romeo's love sees only literally, like a child who pronounces words without getting their meaning. It is Romeo's purely literal understanding of his love that determines its fate throughout the play.

The friar, of course, tries as hard as he can to enlighten the lovers, and make them pause until they can see the meaning of their love. But he fails, partly because the lovers, though they know he is right, cannot *actually* know anything but the love that is moving them; partly because the racing events in feuding Verona prove to be too fast for him. The friar's vision serves to make us understand the death-marked love, but not to cure it.

It would be gratifying to know exactly what Shakespeare read to enable him to transform his source (Bandello's story), lift it to poetry, and see its action in the light of the romance tradition as understood by classical Christianity. That one can never know; but one may recognize the close kinship between Romeo and Juliet and Paolo and Francesca, and see that the two great poets saw the action of romantic love in the same way. The two works throw light on each other, and on the tradition they shared. Dante at the very beginning of the renaissance met it in early youth, Shakespeare at the other end of the renaissance saw it again. Their agreement helps one to understand them both, and also the renaissance, which did not share their understanding of "romance."

III

"Killing the Bond of Love"
Ugolino and Macbeth

THE phrase *killing the bond of love* is taken from canto
11 of the *Inferno*,[1] where Virgil gives his pupil a roadmap
of hell. Virgil says:

> "La frode, ond' ogni conscïenza è morsa,
>   può l'uomo usare in colui, che 'n lui fida,
>   e in quel che fidanza non imborsa.
> Questo modo di retro par ch'incida
>   pur lo vinco d'amor che fa natura.
>
> . . . .
>
> Per l'altro modo quell' amor s'obblia
>   che fa natura, e quel ch'è poi aggiunto,
>   di che la fede spezïal si cria;
> onde nel cerchio minore, ov'è 'l punto
>   de l'universo, in su che Dite siede,
>   qualunque trade in eterno è consunto."
>
> (ll. 52–66 passim)

("Fraud, which gnaws every conscience, a man may prac-
tice upon one who trusts in him, and upon him who places
no trust. This latter mode seems to kill only the bond of
love which nature makes. . . .

In the other mode, the love that nature makes is forgotten, and also that which is added afterwards, creating
special trust. Therefore in the smallest circle, where is the
center of the universe in which Dis sits, every traitor is
eternally consumed.")

Virgil refers to the very bottom of hell, where we shall find Ugolino suffering for his treachery. Macbeth, when he is trying to make up his mind to murder Duncan treacherously, sees his deed in the same traditional terms. He says:

> He's here in double trust:
> First, as I am his kinsman and his subject,
> Strong both against the deed; then, as his host,
> Who should against his murderer shut the door,
> Not bear the knife myself. (1.7)

He sees that the murder would violate not only the natural trust between members of the same species, but the special trust due Duncan as his kinsman and his sovereign and his guest. For Shakespeare as for Dante the act of treachery was the most lethal sin; they both place it at the bottom of the scale of human actions.

The agreement between Dante and Shakespeare, when they both use the same label from the same theology, may seem to "prove" the analogies between their visions of evil. It may do so indeed, if one sees their theology as a map of the concrete wilderness of human motivation. This may show love as ideally binding the human universe together. The countless forms of human love, the motive power of our world, are regarded as more or less inadequate versions of the love of God. Any mistaken action paralyzes or diverts the natural, God-given "movement of spirit," and so damages the harmony of our world; and it is treachery which destroys the harmonious order by destroying the trust that all love must have.

The actions of Ugolino and Macbeth are very similar, and so are the meanings that their authors see in them; but the basis of Shakespeare's *fiction* is eleventh-century Scotland, that of Dante's the postmortem realm of the totally lost. These settings impose different limitations on the two poets, and offer them different resources when they mirror the act of treachery by means of plot, character, and language. I am going to compare the Ugolino episode with *Macbeth*, part by part: the introductory sections, the narrative sequences which display the hopeless condition of the lost soul, and the two scenes of peripety-recognition in which the action is reversed and seen in a wider context.

Descent into Hell

Dante does not show us how Ugolino was originally led into his unrepented acts of treachery; he seems to assume that his readers will know the story. Ugolino was a Pisan magnate caught in the struggles between the Guelfs and the Ghibellines. He was at first a Guelf, but when the Ghibellines grew stronger he betrayed his party to them and their leader, Archbishop Ruggieri. He was then betrayed in his turn by Ruggieri, imprisoned with his sons in the Tower of Famine at Pisa, and left to die there of starvation.

The descent from Hell Gate is designed, however, to lead Dante the traveler, and the reader with him, into Ugolino's prison created by treachery at the bottom of the universe. When Virgil tells Dante (in canto 3) that in hell "the good of the intellect is lost," and when he explains that in the shuddering souls who gather at Acheron to be ferried across, *la tema si volge in disio* ("fear is turned into desire"), he gives clues to Ugolino's actions—and to that of all the lost people. The descent through hell is accomplished, not by Dante's will, but by the will of God, which is felt again and again as the unchanging pull of gravitation. When the travelers at last reach Cocytus Dante knows it as the place where "all the other rocks lean": the center of gravity, in which all movement is paralyzed. So we are prepared to see the ultimate frustration of the psyche which is driven by love, "the movement of spirit," when trust, the bond which love needs, is cut off.

Shakespeare on the other hand must, by the terms of his fiction, account for Macbeth's treachery in Scotland, at a particular moment of history. The play as a whole is composed, like *Richard II* and *Lear*, around the crown, the central symbol of the nation's health or illness. Duncan still has the crown during the first scenes of the play, but his country is suffering the ambiguous atmosphere of the end of the war: "Fair is foul, and foul is fair," as the witches put it. Did the Scots or the Norwegians win the doubtful battle? Which thane of Cawdor deceived Duncan's "bosom interest?" Duncan and all his subjects encounter the bewildering equivocal aftermath of war, but only Macbeth takes advantage of it, or, as we might better say, is taken advantage of by it: led by the witches to misinterpret the "supernatural soliciting" that they relay to him.

From act 1, scene 3, when the witches give Macbeth their double-edged promises, to act 2, scene 4, when all Scotland enters the hellish darkness following the murder, Shakespeare is revealing the growth of Macbeth's treacherous motive within him, under the influence of the witches and of Lady Macbeth; then the murder itself, and finally (act 2, scenes 3 and 4) the entrance into hell. Acts 1 and 2 may thus be regarded as preparation for the portrait of the lost traitor which occupies the rest of the play.

This preparatory movement begins as Macbeth reacts to the witches' prophecy that he will be Thane of Cawdor and then "king hereafter":

> This supernatural soliciting
> Cannot be ill, cannot be good. If ill,
> Why hath it given me earnest of success,
> Commencing in a truth? I am Thane of Cawdor.
> If good, why do I yield to that suggestion
> Whose horrid image doth unfix my hair
> And make my seated heart knock at my ribs
> Against the use of nature?   (1.3)

He sees into himself with remarkable clarity. The high point of this sequence of introspection is reached in scene 7, in the great monologue from which I have already quoted. Macbeth is trying to see what the murder of Duncan would mean:

>   If th' assassination
> Could trammel up the consequence, and catch
> With his surcease, success; that but this blow
> Might be the be-all and the end-all—here,
> But here, upon this bank and shoal of time,
> We'd jump the life to come.

If the murderous blow could end the episode instantly he would neglect his damnation in the life to come:

>   But in these cases
> We still have judgement here, that we but teach
> Bloody instructions, which being taught return
> To plague th' inventor.

And then he sees the murder as the darkest treachery—"He's here in double trust"—the passage I quoted above. He sees that "Pity, like a naked new-born babe,"

> Shall blow the horrid deed in every eye,
> That tears shall drown the wind.

With that vision his murderous drive collapses: "I have no
spur / To prick the sides of my intent"; but Lady Macbeth
is already there to spur him on.

This sequence is a better example than Romeo's introspection of the ability which Shakespeare's tragic heroes
often have of seeing their evil motive clearly even as they
are about to follow it. It is based upon the distinction between actual and potential knowledge, that important bit
of Aristotelian psychology which Dante and Shakespeare
both use frequently. When Macbeth (as in this monologue) really contemplates his coming action in the light
of judgment and of his theological learning, he *actually*
knows it, and is appalled. But when he turns to the daydream generated by his lust for power, he actually knows
only that heady vision, and *la tema si volge in disio* ("fear
is turned into desire").

It is Lady Macbeth who turns him from fear to desire.
She knows how to find in him the right lust, or urge for
power, or obscene combination of the two. Shakespeare
hints at something like that in the sterile erotic relationship
of his two careerists, in act 3, scene 4. But at this earlier point
in the play (act 2, scenes 1 and 2) we see Macbeth con-
centrating on the tour de force of the murder:

> Thou sure and firm-set earth,
> Hear not my steps, which way they walk, for fear
> Thy very stones prate of my whereabout,
> And take the present horror from the time,
> Which now suits with it.   (2.1)

When he has accomplished the murder he does not know
where, or how, to look:

> I am afraid, to think what I have done.
> Look on't again, I dare not.   (2.2)

And then: "To know my deed, 'twere best not know myself."

Scene 3 of act 3 presents the discovery of the murder in various significant lights. The porter, who is conceived in the mood of black farce, lets Macduff and Lennox into the castle where they will soon discover the dead king; and at the same time he lets us, and three types analogous to Macbeth, into Hell: the farmer "who hanged himself on the expectation of plenty" was prevented from profiteering because his crops promised too well; the equivocator who "could not equivocate to heaven" was a Jesuit who falsely swore allegiance to the king to save his religion; and the English tailor who irrationally stole some of the material from an already too-tight French hose. "I'll devil-porter it no further," says the porter as he opens the gate; "I had thought to have let in some of all professions that go the primrose way to th' everlasting bonfire." He then gives Lennox and Macduff an account of his own bawdy wrestling-match the night before with drink, an "equivocator with lechery," that "makes him stand to, and not stand to; in conclusion, equivocates him in a sleep, and giving him the lie, leaves him." We are reminded of Lady Macbeth's scornful question to her husband: "Was the hope drunk wherein you dressed yourself?" The answer, of course, is yes, it was. The Macbeths were as drunk as the porter when they were on their way to hell; the porter offers bodily analogies for their inebriation.

Near the end of the scene Macbeth tries to explain himself. Accounting for his murder of the grooms by his love for Duncan, he unintentionally blurts out the best definition of his action: "Th' expedition of my violent love / Outrun the pauser, reason." The movement of Macbeth's spirit, from the witches' first tempting of him, is clear: his drive for "solely sovereign sway and masterdom" has been too swift for his reason, and has now led him to Hell. It is also evident, if one thinks over the play, that all the characters have been obliged, in the ambiguous atmosphere of the end of the war, to "outrun reason" in their actions. The fainting sergeant who first reported the battle was obliged to strive against all reason in order to speak at all. The king lost his bearings, irrationally overdoing his gratitude to Macbeth:

> O worthiest cousin,
> The sin of my ingratitude even now
> Was heavy on me. Thou art so far before
> That swiftest wing of recompense is slow
> To overtake thee.

Now Macbeth has, by his regicide, deprived his subjects of the light of reason altogether, substituting himself for the mild Duncan in the throne of Scotland, darkening thereby the center by which they had been accustomed to guide themselves. Now everyone who continues to live in Scotland will have to do without "the good of the intellect," accepting the faithless terms of human intercourse which Macbeth has established, just as those who live in a modern police state must do. So all Scotland has become the prison of Macbeth's treachery.

In that very Shakespearean interlude on the morrow of the murder (act 2, scene 4) Ross and the old man, quietly mulling things over, set the stage for Scotland as hell:

> Ah good father,
> Thou seest the heavens, as troubled with man's act,
> Threaten his bloody stage. By the clock 'tis day,
> And yet dark night strangles the travelling lamp.
>
> 'Tis unnatural,
> Even like the deed that's done.

This darkness will prevail in the play until after the turning point in act 4. It serves exactly the same purpose as Dante's *buio d'inferno:* it is a sensuous analogue of intellectual darkness, the state of the damned who have lost the "good of the intellect," the *lumen naturale* whereby we find our way about in the world of nature. And if we can't see the everyday world with its "travelling lamp" our sense of time is gone; Macbeth's race against reason is also a race against time, as he despairingly senses in his great monologue on the brink (1.7). The extratemporal nature of hell is one of its most telling properties in both the *Inferno* and *Macbeth*. Having lost their bearings in time, where mortal man has his only effectiveness, Macbeth and Ugolino are condemned to nightmarish futility, as their stories make clear.

Treachery as Frustration: Ugolino and Macbeth in Hell

I turn now to the stories of Ugolino and Macbeth after they have committed their acts of treachery: Ugolino's narrative (*Inferno* 32 and 33) and acts 3 and 4 of *Macbeth*. It is here that the actions of the two protagonists are most similar: both are trying desperately to accomplish their treacherous purposes, and they cannot see that their efforts must always be in vain.

By the time we reach Ugolino, set in the ice and gnawing the skull of the archbishop Ruggieri, the timeless darkness of the scene, and the *gravezza* which prevails at the center of gravity, have been established; and we have learned that in this region the sinners must fail to get the relief of weeping because their tears are frozen by the terrible cold at the lids, before they can fall. This welling up of unsheddable tears is analogous to the movement of Ugolino's narrative. He first wins our sympathy as he tells us how his sons died of starvation in their Pisan prison, and he then frustrates our need to weep by turning once more to put his teeth to the skull.

Ugolino does not tell us how he had betrayed and then been betrayed in his turn by Ruggieri. He assumes that Dante will know the story, and moreover his aim is to make his auditor sense the cruelty of the death which he and his sons experienced when they were left to starve in prison. He tells us that after he had seen several moons through his prison's little window, he dreamed that he saw the archbishop hunting a wolf and its cubs with swift fierce dogs; and when the dogs caught their prey and started to tear it he was awakened by his sons' crying for bread. It was the hour when they were usually fed, but Ugolino heard the door below fastened shut. To spare his boys, he said nothing. The next day, when he saw his sons' suffering, he bit his own hands in agony, and one of the boys, thinking him hungry, told him to eat them. He calmed himself again to spare them. Between the fifth day and the sixth he saw the boys all die, one by one. He continued to call them for two days after their death; then he too died. We then see him turn his teeth once more—strong as a dog's—upon the bone of the skull; and Dante, speaking out in his own voice, curses Pisa for having permitted the innocent children to starve; and he calls upon the islets Capraia and Gorgona to block up the mouth of the Arno and drown the city.

The little boys are a very important element in the design of this scene. We are touched by them, and we identify ourselves with Ugolino in his terrible need to feed them. We must feel how naturally he is moved by their plight; but at the same time we see exactly how his treachery, which produced their imprisonment, must thwart his love at its source. In his Pisan prison Ugolino's love moved to the surface, like the tears in the preceding canto, and like them was frozen before it could reach its object. In an analogous way our sympathy rises in us, demanding the relief of tears, but is thwarted by the cold savagery of the end of the scene.

The world created by treachery is Cocytus and its inhabitants, but Dante finds that when he crosses it he is obliged to share its mode of being. He has to equivocate, to kick the heads of some of those frozen in the ice, to break his promise. And we are made to feel that treachery may determine the quality of life in a whole city, Pisa or Thebes, just as it puts all Scotland into its hapless prison world, when Macbeth becomes king.

In acts 3 and 4 of *Macbeth* we see the king damned like Ugolino, as his efforts to "complete" his murders, and then to see his way with the witches, prove impotent. Act 3 is devoted to his attempts to get rid of Banquo and Fleance. In scene 1 he invites Banquo to his feast that night, discovers that he and Fleance will be riding through the darkness that very evening, and as soon as Banquo leaves engages two murderers to kill him and his son. In scene 2

Macbeth and his lady agree that "we have scotched the snake, not killed it"; and Macbeth obscurely hints at the forthcoming murders. The third scene shows the two murderers (and a third whom Macbeth had hired because he did not trust the first two) killing Banquo but missing Fleance, who escapes. The fourth scene shows Macbeth's repeated failures to have his feast. He has hardly greeted his guests when the first murderer appears, and he must go to the door to meet him. He learns that though Banquo is dead, Fleance has escaped, and he sees that he has gained nothing: "Then comes my fit again." He tries to return to his guests, but finds the ghost of Banquo (which only he can see) occupying his place. He is appalled, and tries to address the ghost, but only succeeds in alarming his guests. Lady Macbeth tries to reassure him:

> Shame itself,
> Why do you make such faces? When all's done,
> You look but on a stool.

The ghost vanishes, and Macbeth once more approaches his place. But the ghost has returned, and now Macbeth is desperate: "Hence, horrible shadow, / Unreal mockery, hence!" This time he has completely disrupted his banquet, and Lady Macbeth decides to abandon all attempts to go ahead with it:

> At once, good night.
> Stand not upon the order of your going,
> But go at once. (3.4)

When the guests have filed out Macbeth and his lady are left alone. She contemplates him without expressing the despair that must fill her; perhaps she is exhausted. But Macbeth is still engaged in his murderous race against reason, and he resolves to send to Macduff, whom he mistrusts almost as much as Banquo, and to see the weird sisters again on the morrow:

> All causes shall give way. I am in blood
> Stepped in so far, that should I wade no more,
> Returning were as tedious as go o'er.

The whole sequence is very much like Ugolino's eternal efforts to finish Ruggieri. Both poets demonstrate the ultimate impotence of treachery by the simple but effective plot device of the repeated pattern of revealing failure in action.

The visions which the witches show Macbeth in act 4 are analogous to the dreams and visions in the fourth acts of Shakespeare's other tragedies: they are partly erroneous premonitions of the end which we shall reach in act 5. They are unusually full of meanings, some due to their relation to the rest of the play, some to their traditional symbolism. The first apparition, the armed head, obviously signifies Macduff; but it does not dismay Macbeth: it simply confirms his murderous intention. The second, the bloody child, which comes with the announcement that "none of woman born / Shall harm Macbeth" also means that no mortal man shall hurt him. The third apparition, a crowned child with a tree in its hand, means Banquo's seed, but it is accompanied with the false assurance that

> Macbeth shall never vanquished be, until
> Great Birnam Wood to high Dunsinane Hill
> Shall come against him.   (4.1)

Macbeth interprets it as meaning that he will *never* be vanquished. Even in his triumph, however, he is still unsatisfied; and he asks the final fatal question: "Shall Ban-

quo's issue ever / Reign in this kingdom?" The answer is
the nightmarish procession of kings, presided over by Banquo, the last of the repeated patterns of failure. Macbeth
is interrupted in his desperation by the sound of "the gal-
loping of horse," and he learns that Macduff has fled to
England:

> Time, thou anticipat'st my dread exploits,
> The flighty purpose never is o'ertook
> Unless the deed go with it.
>
> . . . .
>
> The Castle of Macduff I will surprise,
> Seize upon's wife, give to the edge o' th' sword
> His wife, his babes, and all unfortunate souls
> That trace him in his line.

He is still trying to outrun reason, now more violently than
earlier.

Except for the procession of kings, the apparitions in this
scene are equivocal, and therefore can encourage Macbeth
to try another action which must fail. They thus correspond
closely to the ambiguous prophecies that the witches gave
Macbeth in act 1. The second and the third also have meanings associated with the play that we have just seen. The
bloody child recalls Lady Macbeth's imagined babe whose
brains she is ready to dash out, and also Macbeth's own "pity
like a naked newborn babe." Its arrival here suggests that
the Macbeths must fail to make Duncan's murder "the be-all
and the end-all": the human generations will continue to
sprout tenderly and innocently, in spite of murder. The
crowned child with a tree in his hand reinforces these meanings and relates them to Macbeth's immediate concern
with the royal succession. This child is not only crowned,

but he carries the ancient symbol of the tree, which is associated with the maypole and with the tree of the knowledge of good and evil in Genesis, which Dante uses in the *Paradiso Terrestre* to stand for divinely sanctioned secular rule and its timeless necessity. It should be noted that each of the apparitions is introduced by thunder, the traditional voice of God; they represent the order of God's world, which Macbeth cannot murder. When the child with the tree tells Macbeth that he will not be vanquished till Birnam Wood moves, the child crazily reassures him; but the next moment the procession of kings returns Macbeth to his unwinnable race.

In *Macbeth* Shakespeare uses children as Dante does with Ugolino—to place the act of treachery in relation to the natural needs of the loving psyche and so bring out its pathos and its horror. Lady Macbeth's suckling infant, Macbeth's pity, the Macduff boy, the infants evoked by the witches, and young Siward in act 5, whose death releases our tears in spite of Macbeth's savagery—all serve like Ugolino's sons to remind us that Macbeth is, or was, a human being, though an evil one.

The Mechanical Impotence of Treachery Recognized

Dante and Shakespeare show their treacherous protagonists as unrepentant, and as unable, therefore, to understand their motives or place them in any human scale. They end their stories of Ugolino and Macbeth with images of their mechanical helplessness unrelieved by any insight on their parts. At the same time they reveal treachery for their audi-

ences by showing peripety and recognition by a participant
or a spectator. *Macbeth* has one ending for Macbeth himself,
and quite another for the play as a whole; and analogously
Dante presents the literal end of treachery in the *Inferno*,
where "the good of the intellect" is lost, and another at the
top of the Mount of Purgatory, where the situation can
reveal treachery and also its meanings.

In the *Inferno* Dante leaves Ugolino grinding away on
the skull with helpless violence, while he curses the city,
Pisa, that permitted such things to occur. The three cantos
devoted to Cocytus, however, are a single unit imitating one
action which deepens as we proceed, and it is in canto 34
that Dante presents the archtraitor, Satan. Satan is the
final image of treachery, including Ugolino's. He is an arti-
fact composed with many meanings: his three faces, red,
yellow-white, and black, for example, represent a travesty
of the Trinity, for he serves as the final set-piece of the whole
hellish journey, corresponding to the literally clear but
mysterious inscription on Hell Gate. He is in himself as lifeless as a road sign, and Dante counts on that very lifeless-
ness to represent treachery as it looks at last. He describes
Satan as though he were discussing a building, recording
dimensions and colors and the wind that comes from the
wings, but making no effort to indicate what Satan's action
may be. When the wings are open enough, Virgil, with
Dante hanging around his neck, proceeds to climb down
Satan's side, clinging to the tufts of hair, and laboriously
turning in the opposite direction when he passes the center
of gravity. When he and Dante climb off and look back,
they can see Satan hanging upside down in the hole through
the center of the earth. One can perceive that Satan, stuck

in that icy realm, chewing Judas, Brutus, and Cassius in his three sets of jaws, and freezing all Cocytus with the wind from his wings, is analogous to Ugolino and the other traitors that we had seen struggling in vain, endlessly repeating their futile gestures. But in order to make Satan the *end* of evil, and to enable us to leave him when we've seen enough, Dante went one step further in portraying him: he made him a lifeless model of the damnation of treachery, reducing him to a mechanism which we may see, when we reach the right point, as harmless in itself like other machines. Because of Satan's position at the end of the *Inferno*, and the knowing symbolism of his parts, there would be a great deal to say about his significance, but perhaps I have said enough to bring out his analogies with Macbeth at the end of *his* story.

It is in act 5, scene 2, when Macbeth is besieged in his castle of Dunsinane, that Shakespeare first finds mechanical metaphors for his condition:

> *Caithness:* He cannot buckle his distempered cause
>   Within the belt of rule.
> *Angus:* . . . Now does he feel his title
>   Hang loose about him, like a giant's robe
>   Upon a dwarfish thief.
> *Menteith:*   Who then shall blame
>   His pestered senses to recoil and start,
>   When all that is within him does condemn
>   Itself for being there?

In the next scene Macbeth sees his own condition that way: "The mind I sway by, and the heart I bear, / Shall never sag with doubt, nor shake with fear." In scene 5, when he hears the cry of women which tells of his lady's death, he says:

I have almost forgot the taste of fears.
The time has been, my senses would have cooled
To hear a night-shriek, and my fell of hair
Would at a dismal treatise rouse and stir
As life were in't. I have supped full with horrors;
Direness, familiar to my slaughterous thoughts,
Cannot once start me.

Very little *can* "start" Macbeth now. He fights until the end,
with savagery but with nothing inside:

Life's but a walking shadow, a poor player,
That struts and frets his hour upon the stage,
And then is heard no more.

Like Ugolino he is blank except for his murderous frenzy;
like Branca d'Oria he is in hell already:

Che per sua opra
in anima in Cocito già si bagna,
e in corpo par vivo ancor di sopra. (*Inferno* 33.155–157)

(Who for his deeds even now in soul bathes in Cocytus,
and above on earth still seems alive in body.)

Macbeth has not yet literally died, but in the last act we
see him confined completely in the hell that his treachery
had created.

Both poets indicate the meanings of their characters' un-
seeing treachery by placing it carefully in the movement of
the whole work. Dante leaves treachery (like all of Hell)
at the literal level of understanding, but he opens up wider
meanings later, when he reaches the Mount of Purgatory
with its earthly light and its divinely placed signs of the
significance of human actions. When he has toiled all the
way up the mountain and seen the tropological meaning

of action in Virgil's classical light, he enters the *Paradiso Terrestre*, and sees visual images of allegorical meaning, the object of faith. The pageant of Revelation brings Beatrice, and his meeting with her is a complex recognition scene in which for the first time he knows his own treachery, and then by the grace of God is relieved of his suffering by being washed in Lethe. This scene is his last ordeal before he can forget the sorrows of earth, where "we are all treacherous," as Ross tells Lady Macduff.

Still on the earthly side of Lethe, Dante realizes that Beatrice is before him, across the stream, and he is as it were removed from the pretty edenic scene, and placed in his own hell, by the contrasting emotions that overwhelm him. He turns, first, to Virgil, to tell him what he sees in the very words lost Dido used to report her fatal passion: *Conosco i segni dell'antica fiamma* ("I know the signs of the ancient flame"); but Virgil has disappeared:

> Ma Virgilio n'avea lasciati scemi
>   di sé, Virgilio dolcissimo patre,
>   Virgilio a cui per mia salute die'mi:
> né quantunque perdeo l'antica matre
>   valse a le guance nette di rugiada,
>   che, lagrimando, non tornasser atre.
>
> (*Purgatorio* 30.49–54)

(But Virgil had left us bereft of himself, Virgil sweetest Father, Virgil to whom for my weal I gave me up; nor did all that our ancient mother lost, avail to keep my dew-washed cheeks from turning dark again with tears.)

Then Beatrice speaks for the first time:

> "Dante, perchè Virgilio se ne vada,
>   non pianger anco, non piangere ancora:
>   chè pianger ti conven per altra spada."

("Dante, because Virgil goes away, weep not yet, weep
not yet, for you must weep for other sword.")

She does not appear as the woman who had gone to Hell for
him, but as the outraged mistress with whom he had broken
faith, and she identifies him literally, by his own name—
the only time his name is mentioned in the *Commedia.*
He looks about, to escape, but in vain:

> Li occhi mi cadder giù nel chiaro fonte;
>   ma veggendomi in esso, i trassi a l'erba,
>   tanta vergogna mi gravò la fronte.   (ll. 75–78)

(Mine eyes drooped down to the clear fount; but be-
holding me therein, I drew them back to the grass, so
great a shame weighed down my brow.)

Dante at this point stands between the perspectives of reason, which Virgil had opened for him, and the perspectives
of faith, which Beatrice has in store. Neither faith nor reason can avail here: he can see only literally, with unmiti-
gated intensity, as he did in hell. He feels the paralyzing
cold of Cocytus itself:

> Sì come neve tra le vive travi
>   per lo dosso d'Italia si congela,
>   soffiata e stretta da li venti schiavi,
> poi, liquefatta, in sé stessa trapela,
>   pur che la terra che perde ombra spiri,
>   sì che par foco fonder la candela:
> così fui sanza lagrime e sospiri
>   anzi 'l cantar di quei che notan sempre
>   dietro a le note di li eterni giri.   (ll. 85–93)

(As the snow amid the living rafters along Italia's back
is frozen under blast and stress of Slavonian winds, then
melted trickles down through itself, if but the land that
loseth shade do breathe, so that it seems fire melting the

candle, so without tears or sighs was I before the song of those who ever accord their notes after the melodies of the eternal spheres.)

Before he hears the singing he cannot get the relief of weeping any more than the treacherous in Cocytus, whose tears are frozen at the lids. He is, however, not actually in the closed realm of Cocytus, but in the *Paradiso Terrestre*, and when he hears the angelic voices the ice about his heart melts:

> Ma poi che 'ntesi ne le dolci tempre
>   lor compatire a me, par che se detto
>   avesser: "Donna, perché sì lo stempre?"
> lo gel che m'era intorno al cor ristretto,
>   spirito e acqua fessi, e con angoscia
>   de la bocca e de li occhi uscì del petto.   (ll. 94–99)

(But when I heard in their sweet harmonies their compassion on me, more than if they had said "Lady, why dost thou so shame him?" the ice which had closed about my heart became breath and water, and with anguish through mouth and eyes issued from my breast.)

The voices were singing the first eight verses of Psalm 31: "In Thee, O Lord, do I put my trust"; and they enable Dante to escape the hell of treachery by recognizing his dependence on God. Beatrice will make him contemplate his sins for another 110 lines, to line 75 of canto 31, rehearsing his philosophic errors as well as his loves, and Dante will suffer every moment of that; yet he is essentially freed from his treachery the moment his flood of tears marks his repentance; for that comes when his hellish isolation is broken by the voices.

Treachery is placed, here, at the very point where Dante's faith in Beatrice—and by way of her in the whole divine

order of his cosmos—is in focus. If he had lost Beatrice—
as he "deserved" to do—he would have lost everything, like
the inhabitants of Cocytus. He does not lose her, because
of the grace that she represents, which appears first as the
ability to recognize his own sin, and then, when he has
crossed Lethe, as the ability to see her beauty: the two aspects of Beatrice are two aspects of one experience of grace.
It is very significant that the whole meeting, with its recognition and peripety, should be separated from Dante's relation to Virgil, and from his own reason and sense of justice. The ultimate meaning of treachery is not tropological,
but allegorical: a matter of *quid credas*. That is why Dante
gives the meeting with Beatrice a mysterious, miraculous
air. The sudden unearned appearance of Dante's despair is
soon followed by the unearned joy of seeing Beatrice, and
both experiences come from without, beyond Dante's will
or his reason.

Shakespeare's scene of recognition and peripety (act 4,
scene 3) is also a matter of faith and grace, not reason. It is
laid in England (corresponding to Dante's *Paradiso Terrestre*) where Malcolm, Macduff, and then Ross meet in
the attempt to combine against Macbeth. Ross prepares us
for it in the preceding scene, in Macduff's castle. In the vain
hope of justifying Macduff's flight he explains to Lady Macduff the hell which is common to all Scotland: "But cruel
are the times, when we are traitors, / And do not know ourselves." Macbeth's treacherous murder of the king has
forced treachery on everyone in Scotland, as the treachery
of Cocytus forces Dante to be treacherous while crossing it;
and treachery must prevent us from knowing ourselves or
each other, make "outrunning reason" the only possible

motive. Malcolm and Macduff have brought the Scottish hell with them to England, and it is against it that they try to meet, until the atmosphere of England, with its divinely sanctioned king, finally penetrates their hellish isolation.

The Malcolm-Macduff scene has three main parts. In the first part Macduff is trying to form an alliance with Malcolm, but Malcolm mistrusts him, for as Malcolm says, "That which you are, my thoughts cannot transpose," and he asks:

> Why in that rawness left you wife and child,
> Those precious motives, those strong knots of love,
> Without leave-taking? I pray you,
> Let not my jealousies be your dishonours,
> But mine own safeties. You may be rightly just,
> Whatever I may think. (4.3)

When Macduff is deeply affronted and threatens to leave, Malcolm makes an elaborate attempt to test him. He tells him that he has more faults than Macbeth himself and that Macduff would make a worse king. Macduff says that he could tolerate his "voluptuousness" and even his "avarice," but when Malcolm claims not to have any of the kingly virtues Macduff despairs:

> Fare thee well,
> These evils thou repeat'st upon thyself
> Have banished me from Scotland. O my breast,
> Thy hope ends here.

At which point Malcolm suddenly disclaims all the vices he had just claimed, and he proposes that they both join the English general Siward against Macbeth. He asks, "Why are you silent?" Macduff replies: "Such welcome and unwelcome thoughts at once / 'Tis hard to reconcile." He echoes the witches' prophecy that "fair is foul and foul is fair" with which the whole play began. He and Malcolm can find no way to meet; they are still in the equivocal hell of Macbeth's treachery.

After this stalemate there is the brief interlude when the doctor appears, to meet the wretched souls who are waiting for the miraculous touch of the king. Their disease is "called the evil," Malcolm explains, and the king has the ability to cure it by touching them:

> With this strange virtue
> He hath a heavenly gift of prophecy,
> And sundry blessings hang about his throne,
> That speak him full of grace.

The whole tranquil little episode may remind us of Duncan's entrance into Macbeth's castle, another interlude in the hellish race:

> This castle hath a pleasant seat; the air
> Nimbly and sweetly recommends itself
> Unto our gentle senses.

It serves, like Dante's *Paradiso Terrestre*, to raise Malcolm's and Macduff's eyes from themselves and their mistrustful confrontation, and to remind them of England and its beneficent monarchy: other possibilities in human life.

The third movement of the recognition scene begins after the doctor's interlude with the entrance of Ross: "My countryman, but yet I know him not," says Malcolm. Then he recognizes him, and returns to the action in a new way:

Malcolm: Good God, betimes remove
   The means that makes us strangers.
Ross: Sir, Amen.

The action is still to recognize and join one's fellows, but now it is conceived in the superrational form of prayer, corresponding to Dante's "In Thee, O Lord, do I put my trust" —the first line of the psalm that he hears sung. Malcolm's conversion, like Dante's, seems to depend upon the interlude which, by the grace of God, broke his isolation. Malcolm is finished with his efforts to join Macduff rationally, and his appeal to God represents a new version of the action of the play, "to outrun the pauser reason." He recognizes the inadequacy of reason in that situation, and the need for an act of faith.

Ross responds with a gloomy picture of Scotland, and then gradually reveals the murder of Lady Macduff and her children. It is the revelation of that terrible event which at last enables all three to recognize themselves and each other, much as Dante's recognition of his own infidelity showed him himself. Macduff says:

> Naught that I am,
> Nor for their own demerits, but for mine,
> Fell slaughter on their souls.

The cold of treachery which had held them apart is dissolved, and all three can join in the new act of faith, the attack on Macbeth. Macbeth had attempted to deny reason altogether, dragging all Scotland into his darkness; but now they have discovered the one action, that of faith, which is both nonrational and good, and they can therefore reverse the course of the play.

It is obvious, I think, that this scene corresponds in several ways to Dante's meeting with Beatrice in which treachery is encountered, recognized, and left behind. Both poets have used characters to recognize treachery who are not hopelessly treacherous like their protagonists, on the ground, I suppose, that we are all treacherous. Virgil, with his classical reason, would perhaps not have thought Dante treacherous to Beatrice, and Dante removes Virgil from the great recognition scene in order to establish the religious nature of his infidelity. Shakespeare is also very careful with Macduff's and Malcolm's treachery. Macduff's consists of course in his leaving his wife and children. Malcolm's is indicated by his long false account of his sins, followed by his sudden reversal of himself. Both poets stage their recognition and peripety outside the scenes created by treachery, and both use the new scenes as crucial elements in the turn to recognition. In both the "recognition" is both the painful one of oneself, and the longed-for one of the person or persons one had been unable to see clearly before. Both poets, as they dismount the world of treachery, enable us to see it in "God's world," where reason can avail once more.

IV

Human Government

Purgatorio 16 and
Measure for Measure

DANTE and Shakespeare had very much the same conception of what the right secular government would be. Shakespeare usually assumes it, rather than expounding it formally; but it has been studied in his histories, his Roman plays, and *Hamlet*, *Macbeth*, and *Lear*. Dante on the other hand expounded it clearly in the *Convivio*, *De Monarchia*, and several years later in the *Purgatorio* in several contexts.

It is essentially a commonsense view, and most readers find it easily acceptable as far as it goes. It does not however have much new light to shed on the problems of government which now face the modern world with its enormous swelling population and its uncontrollably expanding industrial and military power. It envisages a community of human size, in which most citizens might hope to know their ruler and even each other. In Dante's and Shakespeare's tradition it is derived chiefly from Aristotle's ethical and political philosophy, and it naturally assumes (following Aristotle) that ethics and politics are parts of the same topic: the true welfare of man the political animal.

Dante explains it first in the *Convivio*, and then more

fully in *De Monarchia*. The first book of *De Monarchia* is
devoted to the topic of this chapter: the secular state, the
human community as it would have to be in any time or
place. The purpose of secular government, Dante says, is
"earthly felicity" which can be attained only when the human potentialities are fully developed and used. Peace is
necessary for that, and so is the unity of the state. The unity
of the state requires a single ruler, and Dante devoted much
of book 1 to an analysis of the ideal ruler and his role. He
first points out that monarchy (or single rule) is the most
efficient form of government, and then turns to the character
of the ruler himself. He must be free of greed, and wholly
the servant of reason, law, and the good of his people, all
of which means "justice" in the state. In Dante's philosophy
justice is the cure for greed, which he saw as the greatest
danger to the well-being of the community. He identifies
justice with an opportunity for every citizen to follow his
own *real* motive: not his greed, but the fundamental needs
of the human psyche. Justice, therefore, is the guarantor of
freedom. Moreover in the just community under its model
prince true unity will be naturally attained, for the unity
of the state is regarded as the harmony or concord of all its
citizens' wills under their ruler. He writes:

> All concord depends on unity in wills. The human race
> when best disposed is a concord. For as a single man when
> best disposed both as to mind and body is a concord, and
> so also a house, a city, and a kingdom, so likewise the
> whole human race. Therefore the human race when best
> disposed depends upon a unity in wills. But this unity
> cannot be unless there is one will dominating and ruling
> all the rest to oneness; inasmuch as the wills of mortals,
> because of the seductive delights of youth, have need of

a directive principle, as the philosopher [Aristotle] teaches in the last *Ad Nicomachum.* (book 1, chap. 14)

This final vision of the ideal may be regarded as a modest secular version of the paradisal harmony which Dante will explore in the *Paradiso.*

In spite of its medieval language Dante's view contains many of the stubborn commonplaces of political philosophy still, but I disregard that aspect of it because its importance for this book is due to the fact that it expresses the same formal principles which Shakespeare was to use in constructing his great pictures of human communities. Dante's diagrammatic picture of the concord of his ideal state, based on analogies between its citizens' "wills" or actions and the action of its ruler, applies to all of Shakespeare's plays about monarchy. The archbishop of Canterbury in *Henry V*, for instance, describes the unity of England as it is being affirmed for the invasion of France:

> Therefore doth heaven divide
> The state of man in divers functions,
> Setting endeavor in continual motion;
> To which is fixed, as an aim or butt,
> Obedience: for so work the honey-bees,
> Creatures that by a rule in nature teach
> The act of order to a peopled kingdom.
> They have a king, and officers of sorts,
> Where some like magistrates correct at home;
> Others like merchants venture trade abroad;
> Others, like soldiers armed in their stings,
> Make boot upon the summer's velvet buds
>
> . . . .
>
> I this infer,
> That many things, having full reference

To one consent, may work contrariously,
As many arrows loosed several ways
Come to one mark;
As many several ways meet in one town;
As many fresh streams meet in one salt sea;
As many lines close in the dial's centre;
So may a thousand actions once afoot,
End in one purpose.   (1.2)

The archbishop's picture is of course idealized, and it applies to just one jingoistic moment of the national history; but the unity he describes—that of many different but analogous actions clustering around the action of the monarch —is what Richard II, or Claudius, or Lear violates, producing the chaos which is the sign of the tragedy and will last until the erring king is eliminated.

Dante and Shakespeare agree on the ideal timeless rational state, which is for both of them an important norm in their discussion of man's earthly affairs. They also agree that it could hardly be fully realized in any time and place, though Shakespeare gave the Tudors credit for aiming at it. The two works that I now wish to look at, *Purgatorio* 16 and *Measure for Measure*, both dramatize the discovery of the *idea* of the rational community, not its historic realization. They are the only poetic works of their authors that do this; hence their importance and their interest for us.

Purgatorio 16

Dante himself discovered the classical order of ethics and politics after Beatrice's death, when he had fled from Florence to save his life and was living in exile in various north Italian cities, studying and writing under great difficulties.

During this period he read classical literature and philosophy, especially Aristotle, and wrote the *Convivio*, the *De Vulgari Eloquentia*, and *De Monarchia*, works which set forth his view of human life with a classical-humanistic rather than a religious emphasis.

When he came to write the *Commedia* he returned to a strictly religious point of view, and he was ready to find a place for all that he had seen and known. The *Inferno* and most of the *Purgatorio* reflect the experience of his secular classical phase. The *Inferno* shows him as lost, making his way through hell, coping with the powerful figures, the lost souls whom he sees with extraordinary clarity but cannot really place either morally or religiously. In the *Purgatorio* we see him climbing the mountain with Virgil, his guide from the beginning of Hell; meeting various souls who are finding their way; gradually learning to find his own way with Virgil's help. Virgil slowly takes on a fuller and more touching humanity. And in the cantos significantly placed at the arithmetical middle of the whole *Commedia*—cantos 15, 16, 17, and 18—Virgil explains his Aristotelian philosophy of action. This is the climax of Dante's growth in rational understanding, when he gets the trope, or moral meaning, of his postmortem vision of human conduct, all that he can see under Virgil's classical guidance; and it corresponds to the time in his own life when he was reading the classics. The whole four-canto sequence is one unit, marking Dante's first great intellectual achievement on the trip beyond the grave, but I shall endeavor to devote most of my attention to canto 16, which corresponds most closely to *Measure for Measure*.

In canto 15 we climb with Dante and Virgil from the

terrace of the repentant envious to the terrace where anger is purged. Between the specific torments of envy and of anger Dante is comparatively free to think over what he has just seen, and to gather all sorts of fresh intuitions. This canto is filled with analogous lights; the level beams of the late afternoon sun, the glare of the angel of the stairs, who beckons them onward, and various forms of intellectual light which Dante gets from Virgil. Virgil is explaining that material goods must be diminished by being shared, while spiritual goods are increased when shared. Dante as he listens is filled with great but confusing illumination, and the whole experience serves as an introduction to the careful thought of the next three cantos. As Dante is struggling to understand the endlessly suggestive daydreams of gentleness which come to him the light is quenched by a thick fog that makes it impossible to see the way; and so begins canto 16.

Eliot wrote that a single canto of the *Commedia*, rather than the whole poem, corresponds to a play of Shakespeare's. Of course in 140 lines or so Dante cannot present nearly so rich a human context—so many analogous motives —as Shakespeare has room for in a play; but it is true that each canto, like each play, "imitates" one action. It is comparatively easy to see the action of this canto because Dante has used the thick fog which punishes the angry—the *buio d' inferno* ("darkness of Hell"), as he calls it—to unify the action on various analogous levels of meaning. It impedes Dante's progress up the mountain, and because it represents the darkness of spirit which prevents the angry from seeing clearly outside themselves, it punishes them. As soon as Dante asks Marco Lombardo whether mankind or fate is to be blamed for the terrible state of the world we gather that the darkness also represents the condition of Italy from which both Dante and Marco come, and which still makes them angry: *lo mondo è cieco, e tu vien ben da lui* ("the world is blind, and you indeed come from there"), says Marco, with characteristic impatience. In this canto it is Marco, not Virgil, who takes the role of Dante's instructor. Dante chose him, most probably, because he needed someone who had intimate experience of Italian politics to guide him through the contemporary obscurity. The action of the canto is "to get through the darkness"; but as we learn that the darkness is our own condition in anger, and also the darkness of Italy, we realize that to get through it we should have to see some possible cure for the confusion of Italian politics; and Marco not only accompanies Dante through the fog, but he also provides him with the true philosophy of government which frees Dante from the frustrations of his Italy.

The first twenty-four lines of the canto constitute a prologue. The darkness makes Dante cling closely to Virgil; he hears the repentant singing the *Agnus Dei*, and he learns that anger is repented here. Then Marco, who had heard the few words exchanged by Dante and Virgil, inquires who they are. After everyone is identified Marco answers Dante's question about the reason for the corruption of the world, whether the heavens are to blame, or man here below:

> Alto sospir, che duolo strinse in "uhi!"
> mise fuor prima; e poi cominciò: "Frate,"
> lo mondo è cieco, e tu vien ben da lui." (16.64–67)

(A deep sigh, which grief compressed to "uhi!" he first
gave forth, and then began, "Brother, the world is blind,
and you come indeed from there.")

His reply is the main substance of the canto.

Marco first sketches the classic doctrine of the freedom
of the will, which must be the basis of any ethical theory.
Man, he says, is moved to action by all the good things of
earth that he sees around him, but is also vaguely aware of
the Summum Bonum. His subjection to the latter—"the
greater power and better nature"—will enable him, if he
maintains it, to choose among the objects that attract him.
It thus gives him both freedom and responsibility, so when
the world goes wrong he is to blame. Marco proceeds to explain in more detail how this works.

He offers his famous account of the "simple soul" as it
first starts life, meeting the bewildering world:

> Esce di mano a lui che la vagheggia
>   prima che sia, a guisa di fanciulla
>   che piangendo e ridendo pargoleggia,
> l'anima semplicetta che sa nulla,
>   salvo che, mossa da lieto fattore,
>   volentier torna a ciò che la trastulla.
> Di picciol bene in pria sente sapore;
>   quivi s'inganna, e dietro ad esso corre,
>   se guida o fren non torce suo amore.
> Onde convenne legge per fren porre;
>   convenne rege aver, che discernesse
>   de la vera cittade almen la torre.   (ll. 85–96)

(From his hand who loves her before she exists, in the
fashion of a little child that sports, now weeping now
laughing, the simple little soul, who knows nothing, except that, sprung from a joyous maker, willingly she turns

to what delights her. First she tastes the savor of a trifling good; there she is beguiled, and runs after it, if guide or curb turn not her love aside. Wherefore it was necessary to put law as a curb, necessary to have a ruler who might discern at least the tower of the true city.)

This is of course a strictly Aristotelian image of action before it has been complicated by experience and thought: just "the movement of the psyche toward what it sees as pleasing." The guidance of action is the basic problem of government as this tradition saw it: a matter of ethics first of all, the conduct of the individual, but demanding politics the moment that the need of guidance is clear. In the tradition inherited from Plato and Aristotle government was supposed to be responsible for educating and guiding the citizens, leading them to earthly felicity.

Marco continues, placing his simple soul in Italy as it actually is:

> Le leggi son, ma chi pon mano ad esse?
>   Nullo, però che 'l pastor che procede,
>   rugumar può, ma non ha l'unghie fesse.
> per che la gente, che sua guida vede
>   pur a quel ben ferire ond' ella ghiotta,
>   di quel si pasce, e più oltre non chiede.
> Ben puoi veder che la mala condotta
>   è la cagion che 'l mondo ha fatto reo,
>   e non natura che 'n voi sia corrotta.   (ll. 97–105)

(Laws there are, but who putteth his hand to them? None; because the shepherd that leads may chew the cud, but hath not the hoofs divided. Wherefore the people, that see their guide aiming only at that good whereof he is greedy, feed on that and ask no further. Clearly canst thou see that evil leadership is the cause which hath made the world sinful, and not nature that may be corrupted within you.)

Marco goes on to adduce the absolute ("either/or") conflict between the empire and the papacy as the prime example of what *not* to do. One is reminded of books 2 and 3 of *De Monarchia*, where Dante carefully defends the secular authority of the emperors from the absolute claims of the popes. Marco then offers a final picture of the sad state of his country:

> Or può sicuramente indi passarsi
>   per qualunque lasciasse per vergogna
>   di ragionar coi buoni o d'appresarsi.   (ll. 118–120)

> (Now, safely may it be traversed by whomsoever had, through shame, ceased to hold converse with good men, or to draw near them.)

With the mention of three elders who, Marco believes, still have the old virtues, the discourse and the canto end, as light glimmers through the fog ahead.

Marco's explanation to Dante may be regarded as a dramatization of the thesis of book 4 of *De Monarchia:* that we have naturally the power to progress toward the blessedness of earthly life "by the teachings of philosophy, following them by acting in accordance with the moral and intellectual virtues." Marco's philosophizing is in the tradition of Plato and Aristotle. He begins with the myopic either/or question that expresses Dante's impatient state of mind, and leads him, by making distinctions, to see the whole problem in different and much wider terms. Dante's action is to discover from Marco what to blame for the state of Italy that has angered them both, and he expects a simple abstract answer. What Marco gives him is the basis of the classical theory of government, in which there is room both for material determinism and for a gradually attainable ethical freedom. He leads Dante from his total reliance on the discursive intellect to the use of the apperceptive intelligence; from his blind lust for a single final solution to the more charitable acceptance of a complex reality; from the world of the mind, isolated in its darkness and determining everything by logic, to some sense of the real world outside. By such means he frees Dante from his blinding anger and enables him to proceed up the mountain.

But notice that Marco frees only Dante, not Italy: he offers him only a theoretical solution. Dante like Shakespeare believed that true government could be actually attained only by a real ruler, and such a ruler was nowhere to be found when he was writing the *Commedia.* He had thought for several years that Henry VII was the predestined emperor, and when Henry died he was left in despair. It was then that he returned to his religious preoccupations, and when he wrote the *Commedia* he was affirming his view of human affairs in the world beyond the grave, where "God's truth," not man's, prevailed. But in truth—God's or man's —no real ruler was available in his and Marco's Italy, and that is the situation which he shows here. He hears the repentant singing the *Agnus Dei* when he first enters the smoke, and that is the sign of "what he must believe," the faith that will carry him onward when Marco finishes. But the canto as a whole is based entirely on Marco's classical ethics and politics. It is part of that four-canto sequence which sets forth the moral meaning of the journey, and the allegorical meaning will appear only gradually from canto 19 onward.

As the smoke clears at the end of canto 16 the travelers

slowly climb a little farther up the mountain, and Virgil
starts to open up his whole philosophy of action which will
complete the trope. Virgil thus, in a sense, plays the part
of the true ruler, by giving his charge a sense of the mul-
titudinous actions, some evil, some aimed at the good, which
they have seen since hell. His climax comes when in canto
18 he and Dante together contemplate the concept of action
or "love," a moment which represents the blessedness of
this life as reason may reach it. But this too is only theoretical. Virgil will not really represent the true ruler until the
third day of the climb, when Dante realizes that he is the
man who lived and died in Augustan Rome. It is then that
Virgil will stand for the sophisticated Pax Romana which
Dante thought had been the true rule of mankind.

Measure for Measure

Shakespeare wrote *Measure for Measure* about 1604, probably for performance before the new king, James I, rather
than for his more popular audience at the Globe Theatre.
He had recently turned from the long series of his history
plays to his first two tragedies, *Julius Caesar* and *Hamlet*.
One is tempted to think that he was consciously using *Measure for Measure* to outline general questions of human government, much as he had apparently used *The Merchant of
Venice* at the beginning of his series of romantic comedies
to place romantic love in relation to the whole traditional
philosophy of conduct. *Measure for Measure* and *The Merchant of Venice* are both conceived as allegories in the tradition of "medieval realism," which I have briefly described
above.

Shakespeare started this play with a story he had found in an old play, George Whetstone's *Promos and Cassandra.*[1] He changed the leading characters' names to Angelo and Isabella, but accepted Whetstone's basic situation. Angelo is a strict magistrate left in charge of Vienna who, in his efforts to enforce the letter of the old laws, condemns young Claudio to death for seducing his fiancée Juliet before they were married. Isabella, Claudio's sister, in pleading for her brother's life unintentionally awakens Angelo's own lawless passion; and he makes her choose between yielding to him and letting her brother die. Shakespeare brings it all to life, as usual, by endowing his characters with intense individual reality. And he gives the whole play an action quite different from that of Whetstone's play by making Duke Vincentio of Vienna—instead of Angelo and Isabella —the central character.

In the first scene the duke sets up the basic situation of the play by leaving the puritanical Angelo in charge of corrupt easy-going old Vienna. His action, or motive, may be defined by his first line in the play: "Of government the properties to unfold." He foresees that Angelo will try to enforce the old laws which had been long neglected, and that the effect will be to set everyone in Vienna to debating about the true "properties of government." Before act 1 is half over the Viennese of all classes—from Mistress Overdone the bawd, through Claudio, to Isabella and Angelo— have been more or less directly caught by Angelo's rigid policies; and they have all started passionately discussing what government should be from their own diverse points of view. Their actions are, of course, all different, but they are analogous to each other and to what the Duke himself is up to, and together they constitute the action of the play as a whole. It is very much like Dante's action in the darkness of canto 16: to discover what true government would be.

In act 1, scene 3, the duke explains to Friar Thomas why he had decided to leave Angelo in charge:

> We have strict statutes and most binding laws,
> The needful bits and curbs to headstrong weeds,
> Which for this fourteen years we have let slip.

Vienna is in just the condition of Marco's Italy: *le leggi son, ma chi pon mano ad esse?* ("the laws exist, but who puts his hand to them?"). It would have been too severe for the duke himself to start all of a sudden to enforce those laws. Hence he will leave Angelo all his power, and for the time being he will watch incognito in the habit of a friar.

Angelo begins at once to enforce the neglected laws, ordering the whorehouses to be pulled down, arresting Claudio for getting his beloved Juliet with child, and condemning him to death just as the old law demands. Claudio is one of Shakespeare's attractive unregenerate youths who can act only in obedience to their own immediate feelings. So Claudio must have done when he took Juliet, and so he does again now, when he is caught, crying,

> Our natures do pursue,
> Like rats that ravin down their proper bane,
> A thirsty evil, and when we drink we die.

When the duke as friar visits him in prison and advises him to "be absolute for death," he responds wholeheartedly to the duke's wonderful picture of the futility of life, and at that moment prefers death; but a few minutes later, when his sister Isabella tells him he must die to preserve her virginity, he imagines death with sensuous immediacy and shrinks away in horror. He is admirably suited to represent the basic problem of government, being completely in need of guidance and control. He corresponds quite exactly to Marco Lombardo's *anima semplicetta*, the innocent psyche that helplessly obeys its feelings, and is obviously doomed in a society whose leaders, like Angelo, fail to see even "the towers of the true city."

With Claudio established as the central problem for Angelo's government of Vienna, Shakespeare has set up a situation very much like what Marco describes in Italy. But it is characteristic of Shakespeare to present his vision of action in several versions, each with its own point of view. The city setting which he inherited from Whetstone gives him plenty of opportunity for that. In the superb comedy of Mistress Overdone and her lieutenant Pompey, who never consider changing their bawdy profession in spite of Angelo, he exhibits human nature totally incapable of grasping "the properties of government." In Lucio, man-about-town and friend of Claudio, he presents one who, like the Devil, cynically denies all government. It is Lucio who brings Isabella to Angelo to persuade him to relent in his harsh sentence on Claudio, and through Lucio's delighted eyes we see the first round of their debate, when Angelo is erotically moved by Isabella. Lucio had foreseen that Isabella would unintentionally seduce Angelo, and so make a mockery of his judgment, indeed of his whole government.

The great debates between Angelo and Isabella correspond to the dialectic whereby Marco leads Dante to see the possibility of good government, but Shakespeare shows how it fails when the personal relation between the two of them interferes. Angelo wants to stick to the letter of the law, and simply apply the old legal penalty of death to Claudio. He wants "justice" in a literal sense of the word, like the familiar statue of justice with bandaged eyes, holding a scales in one hand and a sword in the other; he assumes that human guilt is abstractly measurable. And having spent his life in the service of literal righteousness, he unhesitatingly condemns Claudio without reference to any of the circumstances. Isabella on the other hand argues for mercy, which always requires us to pay attention to the individual and the surrounding circumstances. She had presumably learned about that in her convent; but as she argues it out she gets excited, and her excitement wakens Angelo's lust. He tells her to return the following day, and in their second scene he gives her the choice between yielding to him and seeing her brother die. That completely upsets Isabella; in her terrible line "More than our brother is our chastity" she decides to let Claudio die to save her from Angelo.

Angelo corresponds to Dante at the beginning of his scene with Marco, when he asked whether man or fate was responsible for human misery. Shakespeare shows that Angelo's faith in his ethical concepts and in his own logic is as strong as though his eyes, like Dante's, had been closed to the real world. When he suddenly decides to obey his lust and possess Isabella at all costs he is still following his absolute temperament: "Blood, thou art blood. / Let's write good angel on the devil's horn." If he can't be absolutely pure he will be absolutely foul. In the first scene Isabella can argue with him in a way which reminds us of Marco's line: she is for that realistic view of the human situation which recognizes actual individuals in all their complexity, and in the intricate situations which surround them; and she rules out government based on a priori concepts. But her sanity cannot quite survive Angelo's direct attack on her, and she is not able to regain her judgment (or her mercy) until the last act of the play. At this point (act 2, scene 4) Shakespeare shows how Angelo and Isabella, who represent the actual leadership of Vienna, cannot by themselves grasp the properties of true government.

The duke in his friar's disguise has been watching the course of events in Vienna, saying nothing. (The reader is reminded that the duke, rather than Angelo, is the central character in the play.) But when the duke learns that Angelo has condemned Claudio to death, and has tried to force Isabella to yield to him, he intervenes—as much as he can as friar—to save the Viennese from the worst results of their follies. He goes to see Claudio and his Juliet in prison, but he leaves them there to repent at leisure. He persuades Isabella to pretend to agree to meet Angelo as he had asked, but to let Mariana take her place in the dark with Angelo. Mariana had been Angelo's fiancée until he abandoned her, and she is still in love with him. By the end of act 3 the secret doings of the friar promise to avert tragedy, but we have a dreary picture of Vienna under Angelo. In a brief scene with Escalus the duke-friar sums it up: "There is scarce truth enough alive to make societies secure, but security enough to make fellowships accursed."

The fourth act represents the slow, frantic, and secret turn from Angelo's rule of Vienna back to the duke's. When the duke (still pretending to be the friar) learns that

Angelo has ordered the execution of Claudio in spite of his
promise to Isabella, he intervenes again, using his ducal
power, for the first time, with the provost of Claudio's prison. This act is mostly set in the prison, and it shows the
duke trying, in spite of several mistakes of his own in judgment, to save Claudio by making the provost send another
head than Claudio's to Angelo. The duke's difficulties are
Shakespeare's inventions; they do not occur in anything he
read for this play. They serve to lengthen the act with
macabre humor, and also to bring out the fact that the duke,
though a ruler, is only a mortal man, without the omnipotence of the God whom he traditionally imitates. He at
length succeeds, with the provost's help, in sending Angelo
the head of a prisoner who had just died. He then, as friar,
tells Isabella her brother was executed, and instructs her
in the role that he wants her to play on the morrow, when
he will return as duke and be met at the city gates by Escalus, Angelo, and all the citizens.

The fifth act consists of the little "courtroom drama"
which the duke had most carefully arranged, in order to
complete the play we have just seen and to demonstrate for
the assembled Viennese the true properties of government.
It moves from a literal vision of Vienna as Angelo pretends
it is to the truth of his regime, when the moral meaning is
clear, and finally to Vienna as it actually is when trans-
formed by the duke's mercy, which brings out the allegorical
meaning.

The playlet begins when Isabella, following her instruc-
tions, loudly accuses Angelo of having possessed her the
night before, and of having nevertheless killed Claudio.
When Angelo denies everything the duke pretends to be-

lieve him, and he orders Isabella held for further questioning. Mariana then interrupts to accuse Angelo of possessing *her* instead of Isabella, and Angelo denies that too, though he admits having been engaged to Mariana five years before. The duke then retires, after sending for the "friar" who was accused of egging the women on, and he leaves Escalus and Angelo to carry on the investigation. There follows a short interlude dominated by Lucio. When the duke returns in his friar's disguise Lucio leads the attack, and the duke-friar defies them all:

> My business in this state
> Made me a looker-on here in Vienna,
> Where I have seen corruption boil and bubble
> Till it o'er-run the stew. Laws for all faults
> But faults so countenanced that the strong statutes
> Stand like the forfeits in a barber's shop,
> As much in mock, as mark. (5.1)

Lucio tries to help the provost arrest the "friar" and pulls off his hood, revealing the duke. Angelo realizes that all is over:

> O my dread lord,
> I should be guiltier than my guiltiness
> To think I can be undiscernible,
> When I perceive your Grace, like power divine,
> Hath looked upon my passes. Then, good prince,
> No longer session hold upon my shame,
> But let my trial be mine own confession.
> Immediate sentence then, and sequent death,
> Is all the grace I beg.

Angelo's desire for literal justice—death—is the final sign of his absolute temperament, and it completes the picture of the moral meaning of his regime.

The duke holds this picture while he makes his judgments according to reason: Angelo is to marry Mariana and then be executed on "the very block where Claudio stooped to death." But Mariana pleads that he spare her husband, and she is joined in a moment by Isabella, in spite of the fact that the latter still believes Claudio was killed at Angelo's order. Isabella has indeed come a long way since saying, in act 1, "more than our brother is our chastity." The duke yields to the intervention of the two women, and so he reveals the allegorical truth of human government: that, after the best efforts of our reason, it depends upon the mercy of God. He admits that he had arranged to spare Claudio; accordingly he now spares Angelo. It then only remains for him to arrange the marriages which conventionally end a comedy. He forces Lucio to marry his punk, urges Claudio and Juliet to marry forthwith, and hints that he himself will marry Isabella.

This routinely happy ending in act 5 displeases some of the play's admirers, for the story of Angelo, Isabella, and Claudio would, without the miraculous intervention of the duke, end inevitably in tragedy. The comic finale is due entirely to the duke, and if one is to accept it—or at least understand what Shakespeare wanted it to mean—one must remember the role of the duke in the whole play. He is of course first of all the Duke of Vienna, an almost diagrammatically good ruler as the ruler was supposed to be: one whose job is to imitate the rule of God as closely as possible. During the first three acts he watches unseen, intervening only with a few hidden acts of "grace": confirming Claudio's instructive experience of awaiting his death, encouraging Juliet in her modest repentance, preventing Angelo from accomplishing his evil purpose of killing Claudio. When he uses his actual all-but-omnipotent power at the end he first brings out the truth of Angelo's rule as only God could see it: "I perceive your grace, like power divine, / Hath looked upon my passes"; and he emphasizes it by judging Angelo in that cold clear light. Not until this result of human efforts at government is clear does he listen to the prayer of Mariana and Isabella. Prayer is required (like the singing of the *Agnus Dei* in the darkness of canto 16) to make us aware of God's rule behind the government which men set up in the free-for-all of actual life. When the duke shows first the true nature of Angelo's rule and judges it, and then his own mercy, he straightens out the affairs of Vienna; but he also reveals the moral and then the allegorical meaning of human government.

The duke must be regarded as a "figure" of God whose meanings emerge only through his role in the changing situations of the play. But in this kind of allegory the figure is not an abstract concept but a real being, and it may therefore mean several things by means of its varied analogical relationships. It is probable, for instance, that Shakespeare intended the duke to mean James I also, the actual ruler of England, known for his theological learning. And the duke is certainly, like Prospero in *The Tempest*, a figure of Shakespeare himself, the author and the director of the play. Shakespeare often thought of the ruler of the theater as analogous to the ruler of society, responsible like him for the truth of his realm. Thus the duke arranges not only the playlet of act 5, but the *whole* play, like a regisseur who sets up the situations for his actors to improvise in, guiding them then with hints, or correcting them when they go wrong. By the time we reach the end of act 5 at least some of these meanings of the duke should be felt, and we should be ready to accept his formal "comic" ending, as he puts away the toys with which he has amused us all evening.

Both Dante and Shakespeare believed that a real man, an actual ruler, was necessary to realize government in the human community. They both indicate that in the works we are discussing, but neither shows such a ruler as actual in history. Dante brings out his concept of government by means of Marco Lombardo, whose discourse raises it up for us out of the actual darkness of Italy. Shakespeare brings it out by means of the duke's demonstration in confused Vienna. But by doing so he raises himself and Vienna, at the end of the play, from history to the realm of theory and belief. The duke is quite unlike the rulers of Shakespeare's history plays and tragedies; they are in history throughout, and it is history, through which God speaks, that ends their tragic careers.

V

Redeeming the Time
The Monarch as "Figura"

IN canto 14 of the *Purgatorio* Dante, in his effort to understand government, discovers the abstract truths of ethical and political philosophy. In *Measure for Measure* Shakespeare also has his eye mainly on those general truths. Both poets are dealing essentially with the timeless problem of government in any time or place, though they make this problem emerge from the concrete situation of Italy or Vienna. Both works stress the trope rather than the allegory, and the texture of both is unusually dialectical.

Both poets, however, knew that the right government seldom or never existed in the actual course of history, and they usually represent it as an object of faith. Dante begins to be concerned with it in this way on the third day of his purgatorial climb when, having absorbed the Virgilian conception of right rule, he begins to realize that he still requires some concrete reality to satisfy him: that theory alone, however true it may be, is insufficient. Virgil slowly emerges as the historic poet of the age of Augustus, when the world enjoyed the right rule of Rome; and this sequence ends at the threshold of Eden when Virgil "crowns and mitres" Dante over himself. Shakespeare deals with the monarch in history in his history plays and in *Hamlet, Mac-*

beth, and *Lear*, in all of which the monarch is a figure of God whose character reveals "the form and pressure" of his time. In both poets the concrete reality of human life, and its allegorical meaning, are stressed in these works, which are concerned with actual history.

In both poets faith in the monarch is considered essential for the well-being of man and his community, because government which depends on the ruler implies a whole order of life. Faith in the ruler and his right government is therefore a religious faith; but both poets, with their theological sophistication, represent that faith realistically, as it might really be found in the people of their time. Thus for Dante Virgil is not God but only a "figure" of God, a particular man who in his visible being can point in the right direction. And for Shakespeare the kings that he portrays, though they represent God in their time and place, lose none of their individual traits. This way with faith, and with the "figures" we use to define it, is characteristic of Dante's and Shakespeare's "medieval realism."

In the *Purgatorio* Dante's faith in Virgil leads him to the *Paradiso Terrestre*, where he sees visions of true rule in history beyond anything that Virgil could have known. In his history plays Shakespeare's faith leads him to the arrival of the Tudors who, in his view, had brought essentially the right government to England. It is obvious that Dante's poem is different from Shakespeare's histories, but the two poets had very much the same conception of the dubious fate of the right government in history.

Dante clearly set forth his theory of government in history in books 2 and 3 of *De Monarchia*. Shakespeare wrote nothing comparable to *De Monarchia*, but recent scholars, especially E. M. W. Tillyard, have explored the sources of his conception of history: the chroniclers, Samuel Daniel's *Civil Wars*, *A Mirror for Magistrates*, and the homilies. I shall consider *De Monarchia* first, and then the sources of Shakespeare's view of English history.

De Monarchia, Books 2 and 3

I have said that Dante and Shakespeare shared the traditional conception of monarchy and its role in history, but Dante was three hundred years earlier than Shakespeare, and must be regarded as one of its early expounders. His *De Monarchia* is a classic exposition of the theory. It is also his clearest work on the subject, for by the time he wrote the *Commedia* Henry VII, the emperor to whom he attached such faith, had died; and he could not, like Shakespeare, represent the true monarchy as actually existing. We shall see how he does represent it in the *Commedia*, but first let us consider the explicit doctrine of *De Monarchia*.

The first book of *De Monarchia* is an essentially Aristotelian account of the rational natural order of human society as it would have to be in any time or place: the natural goal of mankind. It is the duty of the monarch to realize it, that is "to direct the human race to temporal felicity in accordance with the teachings of philosophy." If this is to be achieved all men must be unified, or harmonized, in their aims, which means, Dante believed, that we must have one universal ruler, the emperor. In book 2 he goes on to search for the emperor which history, as the word of God, had indicated. But he sees all too clearly that the unity of the empire no longer exists, that the princes of his time agree "in this alone, to oppose their Lord and his anointed Roman Prince." Hence the task he undertakes in this book: "to show that the Roman Empire existed by right." He knows that this will be difficult to do, for, as he says, he himself had thought at first that the Roman people had gained supremacy "by no right, but merely by force of arms." Only recently has he seen "by most convincing signs that it was divine providence which effected this." He will endeavor to explain this view, seeking to find the invisible will of God by a study of the facts of Roman history.

There are, I think, two main sources of Dante's method of reading Roman history. The first is the biblical tradition that God speaks through history, so that with faith, the Old Testament can be read as the story of the changing relation between God and his Chosen People, a story which leads inevitably to the Incarnation. The second source is the belief, which Dante derived mainly from Virgil, that the providential mission of Rome was to establish the universal authority of Roman law. Thus Roman history, like the history of the Jews, can be read as the word of God, and it too leads to the Incarnation. Dante believed that Rome's pacification of the world was the necessary preparation for Christ, and that God, by placing the Incarnation where he did, and crucifying Christ under the Roman law, had thereby established finally the authority of that law. This paradoxical point is discussed in chapter 13 of book 2, and more fully in *Paradiso* 12. It is perhaps the most striking instance of Dante's care to accept the classical history and literature he knew, as well as the biblical, in his interpretation of the past and its meaning for his own time.

Dante is very scrupulous in defending his view of Rome. He reminds us to begin with of Aristotle's point—that certainty is to be sought only "according as the nature of the subject admits of it." Since he is seeking the will of God, which can be seen only by way of signs, only limited certainty is possible here. He proceeds to remind us of the noble descent of the Romans from Aeneas; the miracles that supported Rome at various moments; the signs that the great Romans were pursuing "the right," which suggests that they already *had* the right; and the overwhelming fact that Rome did actually win supremacy in the known world. The success of Rome in defeating all rivals must, in his opinion, be attributed to Divine Providence, but he devotes a whole chapter to smaller signs of God's intervention which he discovers in Roman history.

The ways in which Dante finds God in history are interesting, because they are so similar to the ways in which Shakespeare's chroniclers find Him there. Some of God's interventions are obvious to reason, but others are hidden and must be divined in various ways: by faith—religious faith; by special grace, sometimes to be obtained by prayer; by studying the Roman wars, and occasional "ordeals" or individual conflicts, which may reveal the will of God if they are properly handled. Dante gives instances of all of these ways of detecting the Divine intention of giving Rome universal authority.

Having established Rome as the one true ruler of the ancient world, Dante proceeds in book 3 to consider the emperor in his own time, that is, after the Incarnation. In this book he is arguing mainly against the ecclesiastics who were maintaining that the church gives the emperor his authority. His own view is that both emperor and pope derive their authority independently from God; that they are separate powers, both necessary. Book 3 is the least relevant to our topic, partly because the separation of church and state has long been achieved, partly because we cannot take seriously the elaborate arguments based on the interpretation of scripture which Dante offers. But the last chapter of this book summarizes his view of the complementary duties of pope and emperor, which are to lead us to our two-fold end: "the supreme pontiff, to lead the human race, in accordance with things revealed, to eternal life; and the emperor, to direct the human race to temporal felicity in accordance with the teachings of philosophy." The pope works in the realm of faith, the emperor in that of reason—which suggests the metaphysical basis of the *Purgatorio* as well as *De Monarchia*.

Dante's aim in writing *De Monarchia* was to clarify the authority of the empire in order to defend it from the popes, and so make possible the secular peace and unity of his world. In this he failed, as everyone knows: the conflict between empire and papacy continued, and Europe was moving farther and farther away from one government as the several kingdoms of the renaissance grew in strength. Yet the principles Dante used to define his universal monarchy and to justify it historically served in the next generations to support the religious kingdoms of France and of England. That was the tradition Shakespeare inherited through writers in his own country.

Sources of Shakespeare's View of the Monarch in History

We owe our current notions of Shakespeare's philosophy of the monarch in history largely to E. M. W. Tillyard, who carefully studies its sources in his important book *Shake-speare's History Plays.* Tillyard first explains Shakespeare's adherence to the medieval conception of order—in the individual, in the state, and in the cosmos. He illustrates with quotations from the plays, especially from Ulysses' great speeches in *Troilus and Cressida.* Shakespeare often thought of the king as analogous to the sun, the center of human affairs as the sun was taken for the cosmic center. Tillyard then proceeds to sketch various works which elaborate a conception of English history very much like Shakespeare's: Froissart, Spenser's historic myth, Polydore Virgil, Sir Thomas More, and Hall and Holinshed. From these and other writers there emerged a conception of recent English history, the period of the Wars of the Roses from Richard II to Henry VII, which Tillyard calls the Tudor myth. The whole period of civil war was taken as an organic sequence, whose triumphant conclusion, when the Tudors won the throne and introduced the peace and prosperity which culminated with Elizabeth, was due to the providence of God. The Tudors, beginning with Henry VII, were divinely destined to save and pacify England.

If one reads *Richard II, Henry IV* 1 and 2, *Henry V, Henry VI* 1, 2, and 3, and *Richard III*, in that order, one can see that Shakespeare in this sequence was indeed dramatizing the Tudor myth and that he must have gotten it from the authors Tillyard studies. He assumes with them and the great majority of his educated contemporaries that the country must have the right monarch to keep it in order at home and defend it from enemies abroad. And he assumes that God provides the monarch, whether a good one to save, or a bad one to punish, the people; he reads history as the chroniclers did, in the faith that God spoke through it. Tillyard points out that this pattern is completely absent from nearly all the "chronicle plays" which were popular in Shakespeare's time. "It is this absence from them and its presence in Shakespeare," he adds, "that should teach us to link him not with the less educated writers of plays but with the best educated and most thoughtful writers outside the theatre as well as within."

Tillyard investigates also a number of other works which nourished Shakespeare's vision. They help one appreciate the fact that for Shakespeare the right monarchy was the realization of the whole Elizabethan sense of moral and religious order. They include the epic poem by Samuel Daniel on the rise of the Tudors, Daniel's *Civil Wars between the Two Houses of York and Lancaster; A Mirror for Magistrates*, and the Books of Homilies of the Church of England. These three works were popular, Tillyard says, and expressed the orthodox view of recent history, of the monarch, and of the dangers of rebellion. It is thought that Shakespeare certainly knew and accepted them all.

One can see quite easily, I think, that the works studied by Tillyard are in the same tradition Dante was in when he wrote *De Monarchia*. They assume that monarchy is the divinely ordained right rule for mankind, that monarchy demands a real man to be king, and that God must somehow, soon or late, provide him. They read English history as Dante read Roman history: in the faith that God spoke through it. And they accepted the same things that Dante did as revealing God's will: not only the historic sequence itself, which led to the Tudors, but the characters of some of the kings, notably Henry VII's justice; extraordinary, perhaps "miraculous" events; great battles; and a few "ordeals" which God was supposed to have decided. They differ from Dante because they are defending an existing monarchy instead of the theory of its necessity. Tillyard writes: "Here in Hall we get the full transfer of historical drama from the sacred to the secular while what is lost from sheer worship of God is used to make sterner the pious morality governing profane events." The chroniclers and Shakespeare do devote most of their attention to the "profane events" of history, but in doing so they are governed by the "pious morality" of the traditional faith. They seem to have been determined to *realize* the traditional faith, and therefore had to focus on actual events. But at the same time they had to see the people and the deeds they treated as having another dimension: occurring not only in time but also in the timeless drama of God's will for man. When the course of history at last produces Henry VII they praise God for the whole sequence. In short, for a generation or two before Shakespeare, the English had been applying doctrines very much like those of *De Monarchia* to the structure and recent history of their own country. It was their vision that Shakespeare inherited and used as the basis for his plays.

The True Ruler in the *Purgatorio*

In studying Dante's quest for the true ruler in the *Purgatorio* one must remember that he didn't believe the true ruler existed in his time; and one must remember (as I pointed out when considering *De Monarchia*) that ethics and politics were parts of the same topic—total human welfare. The right monarch would produce order in all of human life; the wrong monarch would produce disorder there. The quality of the monarch determines "the age and body of the time, his form and pressure"; and as Dante encounters the varied qualities of different historic moments he sees them as due to good or bad rulers. His quest for the true monarch is thus inseparably connected with the state of the world as he sees it, especially in his Italy or in Augustan Rome.

That is all assumed in the great lament that he utters on the state of Italy in his own time, near the end of the *Antipurgatorio*[3] (canto 6). He and Virgil have been wandering, lost, among the foothills of the Mount of Purgatory, when late in the day they meet the poet Sordello. Sordello and Virgil embrace when they discover that they are both Mantuans, and their deep concern for each other and for their country inspires Dante to make his great tirade on the lost condition of Italy:

> Ahi serva Italia, di dolore ostello,
>> nave sanza nocchiere in gran tempesta,
>> non donna di provincie, ma bordello!　　(ll. 76–78)
>
> (Ah Italy enslaved, hostel of misery, no princess among the provinces, but a brothel!)

He attacks the people for being without faith or peace, relentless fighters among themselves, because no one obeys the emperor, and the clergy have seized the reins of power. He bitterly reproaches the emperor "German Albert" for abandoning his responsibilities. The Italian cities, he says, are all filled with tyrants, for every clown who plays politics becomes a "Marcellus," that is, a demagogue hostile to the emperor. He comes at last to Florence, which he attacks with irony, grief, and scorn. The seventy-five lines of this outburst mark the dark end of Dante's search on earth for the true ruler. They remind one of the curses and laments which resound in Shakespeare's history plays when the failure of the king produces chaos in the state and in the individual.

Such is the all but hopeless situation in Dante's own time and place. But during the second day of his purgatorial journey beyond the grave he begins to see better possibilities for the true rule of humanity. The path is filled with signs that point the way, and in canto 15 Virgil begins to use them to enlighten Dante about the meaning of their experiences. We have already noticed that in cantos 15–18 Virgil opens the whole Aristotelian conception of the order of human life. In so doing Virgil is playing the role of the ideal monarch as Dante understood it. In answering Dante's questions he presents the perpetual possibility of true order: what philosophy might still guide us to, if we were able to follow it where it leads.

But after the climax of Virgil's philosophizing in canto 18 Dante, overcome by the weariness of his body, sinks into uneasy sleep, a sign that he is returning to the more normal human consciousness—no longer concentrated on Virgil's general truths, but aware of the body and its needs for food and love. Virgil himself, in cantos 19–30, will appear more and more strongly as the actual mortal man who had lived and died in Augustan Rome. In Hell and during the first day in Purgatory he had impressed Dante as the all but omniscient and omnipotent guide—much the way a loved parent impresses a young child. But now his limitations as one who had lived in this historic period before Christianity will be felt, as Dante begins to need what Christian love will offer him. During this third day of the climb Virgil is a figure of the true rule of Augustan Rome as it paradoxically appeared to Dante: the necessary preparation for earthly felicity (as he had explained in *De Monarchia*)—the best man can do short of Revelation. Yet at the same time we are continually reminded that Virgil will not be able to see the Christian scheme which begins in the *Paradiso Trerestre*, and, moreover, that his true rule was *realized* only temporarily in Rome. It now looks more and more ghostly as Virgil himself does. When the true ruler—Augustus or Virgil himself—is dead and gone, true rule, "true" though it be, cannot be real for us.

During the third day Virgil continues to lead his charge toward the revelation that awaits him, but without knowing himself what it means. His role is thus closely analogous to what Moses's was traditionally supposed to be: that of "a schoolmaster to bring us to Christ"—and a "figure" of Christ in the Christian scheme. It is very characteristic of Dante to have made the classical Virgil, like the Hebrew Moses, a figure of Christ. As a "true ruler" he would have had to be a figure of Christ, for that was one of the things the divinely sanctioned king was supposed to be. But a figure is different from what it stands for; Virgil is not Christ; and Dante uses the analogy to build the pathos of Virgil's plight as he approaches the moment when he must return to limbo.

The great recognition scene in canto 21 between Virgil, Dante, and Statius—the Roman poet who overtakes the travelers on their upward climb—brings out some of these Virgillian qualities. When Statius at last realizes who Virgil is—the man who had first taught him to be a poet—he tries to clasp his knees, and fails because Virgil is only a shadow. He has forgotten their "vanitate" as he puts it: that here beyond the grave they lack the full human reality of soul *and* body, and that the human state, anyway, is shadowy compared with Being itself, which Statius is supposed to be seeking; and that Virgil, beloved as he is, is only, ultimately, a sign or figure.

When Virgil responds to Statius' homage at the beginning of canto 22 he explains the psychology of their supra-temporal communion: *Amore, / acceso di virtù, sempre altro accese, / pur che la fiamma sua paresse fuore* ("Love, kindled by virtue, always kindles another, provided its flame appear outwardly"). Using Dante's formula for true poetry as the inspiration of love, one might paraphrase as follows: the love that Virgil heard within himself and that was signified outwardly in his poem kindled Statius' love when he read the poetry properly and so inspired his own poetry. Dante more than a thousand years later was fired by the *Aeneid* in a similar way, and that is why he can join the conversation here, redeeming his own dark time, and sharing the high pagan awareness of Augustus' regime on the eve of the Incarnation.

Statius tells Virgil that he led him not only to poetry but to Christ, and he quotes a bit from Virgil's prophetic Fourth Ecologue, which was often taken in the middle ages as an obscure premonition of Christianity:

> "Secol si rinova;
> torna giustizia e primo tempo umano,
> E progenïe scende da ciel nova."
>
> (*Purgatorio* 22.70–72)

(The age turns new again; justice comes back and the primal years of men, and a new race descends from heaven.)

But Virgil never saw and never will see the love of God Incarnate, as both Statius and Dante will, and so (in Statius' famous image) he is like a man going through the dark, carrying a light behind him, and so benefiting those who follow him but not himself. Virgil did not see his empire as a preparation for Christ any more than Moses saw the law that way; and so, as we come closer to earthly felicity, we encounter things that Virgil cannot fully explain.

The tree which the travelers meet here was, as we learn later, taken from the tree of the knowledge of good and evil which grows in Eden, a very ancient symbol or icon or totem. Modern studies lead us to think that it was a tribal totem before it appeared with the familiar interpretation in Genesis. Dante stages it here in such a way as to make it feel ancient, and ultimately unsoundably mysterious. It is fresh and green, filled with delicious smelling fruit, and sprayed from a waterfall: but it is not to be climbed, having few branches at the lower level; and the poets hear a voice in the leaves saying: "Of this food you shall have scarcity." Such is its literal reality; but we go on to learn its moral meaning, and then its allegorical significance, which is dependent on the faith that Virgil does not appreciate.

It is, as I have mentioned several times, characteristic of Dante's method that he gives us the literal reality first, and then (like corollaries) the moral meaning of its inaccessible attractiveness, and finally the allegory. Our first impression is like that of the totem we read about in many anthropological works: it is both attractive and forbidden, desirable but sacred and taboo. We then learn its moral meaning: it is here to tempt and thwart the repentant glut-

tonous. Virgil accepts that at once, and invites Dante to
proceed with his climb, as though the evident *moralis* were
all there was to see:

> "Figliuole,
> vienne oramai, ché 'l tempo che n'è imposto
> più utilmente compartir si vuole." (23.4–6)

(Son, come on now, for the time appointed us must be
put to better use.)

But then Dante hears the repentant singing with both pain
and delight; he sees their terrible emaciation, and then he
meets his old friend Forese Donati. Forese interprets the
tree not morally but allegorically:

> Tutta esta gente che piangendo canta
> per seguitar la gola oltra misura,
> in fame e 'n sete qui si rifà santa.
> Di bere e di mangiar n'accende cura
> l'odor ch'esce del pomo e de lo sprazzo
> che si distende su per sua verdura.
> E non pur una volta, questo spazzo
> girando, si rinfresca nostra pena:
> io dico pena, e dovria dir sollazzo,
> ché quella voglia a li arberi ci mena
> che menò Cristo lieto a dire "*Elì*,"
> quando ne liberò con la sua vena. (ll. 64–75)

(All these people who weep as they sing, having followed
their appetite beyond measure, regain here in hunger and
thirst their holiness. The fragrance which comes from
the fruit and from the spray that is dispersed over its
verdure kindles in us the craving to eat and drink, and
not once only our pain is renewed as we go round this
level; I say pain and ought to say solace, for that will lead

us to the tree which led Christ gladly to say Eli, when with his own veins he freed us.)

Virgil makes no comment, the moral interpretation of this tree suffices him, just as the moral interpretation of true rule sufficed him when he explained it in canto 18. His only answer to that "natural thirst" which is now driving Dante and Statius swiftly upward is ascetic control. Virgil must live forever, soberly and decently, but sadly, in his castle in Hell: "in desire but without hope," as he puts it. He does not see the Christ who by his sacrifice turned the necessary discipline of government from pain to solace.

Virgil however accompanies Dante and Statius the rest of the way to the *Paradiso Terrestre*, for in Dante's view the enlightened freedom of Augustan Rome led both to earthly felicity and to the Incarnation. When Dante has to cross the wall of flame guarding Eden (canto 27), Virgil fails to persuade him to undergo that suffering until he reminds him with affectionate irony that Beatrice is somewhere beyond the flames. When Dante ventures in, thinking only of Beatrice, we see him moved for the first time by faith alone, his faith in Beatrice instead of by his usual confidence in Virgil and his reasons. When the travelers wake near the entrance to Eden, Virgil speaks for the last time, giving Dante full authority over himself, and so completing his own task as true ruler:

> "Il temporal foco e l'etterno
> veduto hai, figlio; e se' venuto in parte
> dov'io per me più oltre non discerno.
> Tratto t'ho qui con ingegno e con arte;
> lo tuo piacere omai prendi per duce:
> fuor se' de l'erte vie, fuor se' de l'arte.

. . . .

Non aspettar mio dir più né mio cenno;
    libero, dritto e sano è tuo arbitrio,
    e fallo fora non fare a suo senno:
per ch'io te sovra te corono e mitrio."   (27.127–142)

("Son, the temporal fire and the eternal hast thou seen,
and art come to a place where I, of myself, discern no
further. Here have I brought thee with wit and with art;
now take thy pleasure for guide; forth art though from
the steep ways, forth art from the narrow. . . . No more
expect my word, nor my sign. Free, upright and whole is
thy will, and 'twere a fault not to act according to its
prompting: Wherefore I do crown and mitre thee over
thyself.")

Virgil assumes that, having undergone the whole rational
discipline, they are due to enter "earthly felicity" in the classic sense. When they start exploring the *Paradiso Terrestre*
it does indeed look like the "Golden Age," and Virgil seems
to recognize it. Only when the pageant of Revelation has
brought Beatrice (canto 30) does Dante realize, with dismay, that Virgil is gone. For the rest of the poem he will
have to see visions of Christianity and of Christian history
not only without Virgil's reason but without his presence.
What these visions contain is the allegory "what you must
believe." With Virgil's disappearance classical right rule,
which regulates human life on earth, ceases to be relevant,
for Dante by the grace of God is being prepared to explore
the supernatural realm of paradise.

    It is in this second part of the *Paradiso Terrestre*, after
Virgil's departure and the crossing of Lethe, when we see
Eden as it has been since Adam's fall and redemption, that
we meet the tree of the knowledge of good and evil from

which the trees of the terrace of gluttony were taken. It is enormously tall, and being despoiled of leaves, it looks dead and wintry. As we approach it we hear the word *Adam* murmured, which reminds us that Adam violated it by tasting of its fruit against the command of God. As the car drawn by the griffon (Christ) approaches the tree we hear:

> "Beato se', grifon, che non discindi
>   col becco d'esto legno dolce al gusto,
>   poscia che mal si torce il ventre quindi." (32.43–45)
>
> ("Blessed art thou, grifon, that with thy beak dost rend naught from this tree sweet to taste, since ill writhes the belly therefrom.")

The griffin replies, "Sì si conserva il seme d'ogni giusto" ("So is preserved the seed of all righteousness" and attaches the helm of his car to the tree. The tree at once puts forth foliage like that of a supernal spring, while heavenly music is heard. Dante is overcome, like the disciples at Christ's transfiguration; and he sleeps.

These visions, like all of those in the *Paradiso Terrestre*, are packed with unexplained meanings, partly because of the fact that they are all ancient, and had been interpreted in various ways in the long course of Dante's tradition, partly because of the richly significant contexts in which they appear. It is clear that the tree represents rule, or empire, in the most general sense, as Beatrice explains in the last canto (lines 56–72). The tree when it looks dead stands for empire after Adam's initial sin, and Christ's attaching his car to it, and its miraculous flowering, shows what it could have been after Redemption. But when Dante wakes after that beatific vision he sees nightmarish attacks on the tree and on the car of the church by an eagle, a fox, a dragon, a giant, and a whore, which obscurely represent the vicissitudes of church and state up to Dante's own time. His doctrine of the relation of church and state in history is clearly outlined in *Paradiso*, cantos 6 and 7, but instead of considering that, I wish to return to the tree, or trees, as they appear here in the *Purgatorio*, for the actual tree, mysterious though it is, is more relevant to Shakespeare's vision of monarchy in history than the theological disquisitions of the *Paradiso*.

The first appearance of the tree in canto 22 establishes its literal reality, which underlies and sustains the meanings that it acquires in subsequent appearances. It is simply a tree with tempting fruit, like such trees as we may see around us: a natural growth seeming full of promise for us, yet impossible to climb. Being both attractive and forbidden it is like a totem, and these qualities also account for its function here, which is to tempt and thwart the repentant gluttonous. What is forbidden is probably not only the pleasure of eating its fruit but the knowledge of good and evil which comes to whomsoever tastes it. When Virgil, satisfied with its moral meaning, tells Dante to leave it instead of lingering to satisfy his curiosity, he seems to renounce (as he does several times in the *Purgatorio*) the natural thirst for religious (as distinguished from rational) knowledge. We shall learn later that the tree stands for human government, and Virgil's attitude toward it shows his classic view of empire. It is (as we have seen) Forese Donati who explains its religious meaning by analogy with Christ's joyous-painful sacrifice, and so transforms the renunciations demanded by any government into an act of religious love. All of this prepares us to meet the original of this tree, in Eden: the tree of the knowledge of good and evil itself.

And it enables us to understand better Adam's sampling the knowledge of good and evil, which subjected him to the restraints which any government since has had to impose on humanity. So the tree has acquired a succession of meanings in the historic sequence as Dante understood it: the moral meaning which the Hebrews attributed to their totem, and at last the meaning it should have in the light of Christian revelation: human government as a figure of the way to God, fresh, living and desirable as spring itself.

Shakespeare was aware of the poetic and dramatic possibilities of the tree as symbol of rule, and he used them especially in the trees Macbeth sees when in act 4 the witches show him a picture of his fate.

Shakespeare's Monarch in History: *Richard II* and *Lear*

Shakespeare, as we have seen, took the theme of the monarch in history most directly from the chroniclers who had made the "Tudor epic." Their theme, the rise of the Tudors, governs the plays devoted to the Tudor epic itself: *Richard II*, *Henry IV* 1 and 2, *Henry V*, *Henry VI* 1, 2 and 3, and *Richard III*. In *Hamlet*, *Macbeth*, and *Lear*, he is of course not concerned with the Tudor epic—the history he treats is more remote than the recent history of England—but his view of the monarch in history is the same, and he handles it even more completely and with even richer insight. He has in his reading a great deal of concrete material to work with, and he had the tangible, visible regime with its ceremonies and its pagaentry before him in London. His audience moreover was ready and eager to watch the bloody history of the crown, which had ended so fortunately in their own time. They would have understood instinctively, and shared, the action which each of the plays has in its own way: "to secure the right rule for England."

Shakespeare seems to have been the only playwright who fully understood what the figure of the monarch had for the theater. For he alone made full use in his plays of the king's symbolic significance: analogous in human society to the sun in the cosmos; the chief sign of God's will in history; the man who in his acts of rule made "the age and body of the time, his form and pressure"—in other words the center of society and the clue to its good or bad quality. This is in complete agreement with Dante's vision of the ruler, but where Dante could realize it only as he discovered it in his postmortem purgatorial journey, Shakespeare had it before him in the swarming history of England, and in the structure of his own society.

Richard II clearly shows the basic scheme of all the histories, each of which is named for a king who gave his time its form and pressure. Richard, the last of the Plantagenets, had the full, if overliteral conception of the king; and Shakespeare gives this play a more medieval tone than the others. The dethronement of Richard by Bolingbroke marks the start of the Wars of the Roses, which Hall and Daniel had made into the Tudor epic. It has some sense as an independent play, but much more when considered as part of the whole triumphant sequence ending in *Richard III* when Henry VII at last dethrones Richard. For the eventual success of the Tudors must be kept in mind if one is to get the meaning Shakespeare saw in *this* act of his eight-play "epic."

The play opens with a ceremonious meeting before King

Richard, which suggests the patriotic motive: the welfare of England which depends upon the crown. We learn at once that England is threatened by the quarrel between the powerful dukes, Bolingbroke and Mowbray, who are accusing each other of treason; and we look to Richard to settle the matter, for that is his job as the actual, legitimate, and divinely sanctioned ruler. But he proves inadequate to the task. He can't quiet the dukes, and he eventually allows them to challenge each other to mortal combat; yet when they appear (scene 3) for their ceremonious ordeal he stops the fight and banishes them both, Bolingbroke for ten years and Mowbray for life. This failure of Richard's is the beginning of the tragic action of the play. By the end of act 3 Bolingbroke has returned from exile to protest Richard's confiscation of his property, and he has taken over most of the kingly power and most of the kingly duties.

The basic duty of the king is of course to see that reason and justice prevail in the body politic. That was well understood by everyone: the king must lead the community, by the exercise of his moral and intellectual virtues, toward earthly felicity, which is figured in Eden. Shakespeare does not feel obliged to dwell very much on the essential but routine duties of rule, which (he makes us feel) Bolingbroke is much better fitted to discharge than Richard is. In accord with the medieval tone of the play, however, he keeps Eden, ancient figure of earthly felicity, before us in various ways. The dying Gaunt (act 2, scene 1) sees England as having been Eden before its present troubles: "This other Eden, demi-paradise"; but now as "leased out . . . like to a tenement or pelting farm." When the queen (in act 3, scene 4) watches the old gardener at his work, both of them are reminded that England *should* be Eden, though they interpret that parable in contrasting ways. The gardener thinks that Richard, like a negligent ruler, has let the goal of England's felicity be lost to sight, and he proceeds to prune and weed his garden, lamenting that Richard has not done the like in the "garden" of England, for the weeds he neglected have grown so large that they have overthrown him. The queen interrupts in despair:

> Thou, old Adam's likeness set to dress this garden,
> How dares thy harsh rude tongue sound this unpleasing
> news?
> What Eve, what serpent hath suggested thee
> To make a second fall of cursed man?

The gardener has playfully pretended to be Richard cleaning the garden of England to make it look like Eden, but the queen takes him as Adam, who originally lost Eden by rebelling against God. She seems to assume that Richard is not only the earthly figure of God but God himself—an error that Richard tends to make in the early scenes of the play. The scene as a whole, with its flowers, its rhymes, its quiet atmosphere, reminds one of an illumination in some pious medieval book.

Shakespeare's central interest, however, is, as usual in his histories, in the terrible difficulties which must ensue when one tries to take a mortal man as the figure of God. This conception of the king was no doubt necessary in order to establish the monarchy, but its difficulties were familiar and often encountered. Kantorovich explored some of them in his erudite book, *The King's Two Bodies*, as they crop up in about four hundred years of jurisprudence and constitutional law. How is one to understand the mysterious re-

lation between the king as an individual man and the king
as the figure of God? Shakespeare's histories always start
with a king who is not right for his exalted meaning and
who therefore creates an insoluble problem: that of getting
rid of him without at the same time destroying the authority
and the moral and religious significance that he embodies.
That is just the problem in *Richard II.* By the end of act 3
the insoluble difficulty has divided all men of good will in
themselves, and the whole body politic in *it*self. Even Richard, embarrassingly childish as he has been, now begins
in a helpless but deeply imaginative fashion to realize his
true situation.

When Bolingbroke catches him at Flint Castle (act 3,
scene 3), his attempt to establish himself as king consists
in an inspired histrionic effort to *act* the part. The theater
director Richard Boleslavsky used to tell his actors that the
king was the easiest role to play on stage because it was up
to the other actors to create his kingliness by calling him
"Sire," kneeling when he appeared, swelling his progresses,
and the like; Shakespeare's kings depend on the faith and
the ritualistic make-believe of their subjects to exist as kings;
and when Richard has to face the rebellious Bolingbroke
he tries to give him the clue histrionically. Bolingbroke, in
the basse-cour of the castle with his army, sees Richard
appear high above him on the wall:

> See, see King Richard doth himself appear,
> As doth the blushing discontented sun
> From out the fiery portal of the east,
> When he perceives the envious clouds are bent
> To dim his glory, and to stain the track
> Of his bright passage to the occident.

Richard certainly wishes to assimilate himself to the sun, traditionally a figure of God in the cosmos as the king was God's figure among men. His first speech is in accord with his role as God's anointed deputy:

> We are amazed, and thus long have we stood,
> To watch the fearful bending of thy knee,
> Because we thought ourself thy lawful king.

Bolingbroke and his ally Northumberland don't leave, but make their demands; and Richard perforce descends, acting out as he does so the cosmic fall of Phaethon: "Down, down I come, like glistering Phaethon, / Wanting the manage of unruly jades." That is in effect the end of Richard's kingly rule.

Act 4, scene 1 shows Richard's formal abdication. It is one of the places where Shakespeare presents Richard most subtly. He characteristically abdicates without really abdicating, for he deeply feels that since he has been appointed by God abdication is impossible. He plays variations on such themes as his appearance versus the reality of his situation, his power versus his impotence, belief versus make-believe. Richard has come a long way since act 1. His rich imagination has plenty to work with, and he gives us a many-sided picture of the sacrilegious event as it must have struck its prime victim. His scene however follows that in which the bishop of Carlisle sturdily defends him. The bishop presents the full weight of the traditional doctrine of kingship, as it bears upon the immediate legal and constitutional problem of getting rid of the legal king:

> What subject can give sentence on his king?
> And who sits here that is not Richard's subject?

Thieves are not judged but they are by to hear,
Although apparent guilt be seen in them,
And shall the figure of God's majesty,
His captain, steward, deputy elect,
Anointed, crowned, planted many years,
Be judged by subject and inferior breath
And he himself not present?

The bishop is saying, like the homily of the English church
which Shakespeare heard as a child, that insurrection against
the true king is impossible, no matter what the king does.
And he goes on to prophesy the vengeance of God, which
Shakespeare's audience, remembering their civil wars, knew
to be true:

My Lord of Hereford here who you call king
Is a foul traitor to proud Hereford's King,
And if you crown him let me prophesy,
The blood of English shall manure the ground,
And future ages groan for this foul act.
Peace shall go sleep with Turks and infidels,
And in this seat of peace tumultuous wars
Shall kin with kin, and kind with kind confound.

His vision of the chaos which must follow when the right
king is gone corresponds exactly to what Dante sees in Italy
when the emperor is missing. I quote from the great monologue in *Purgatorio* 6 which I mentioned in the last section:

e ora in te non stanno sanza guerra
li vivi tuoi, e l'un l'altro si rode
di quei ch'un muro e una fossa serra.

. . . .

Ahi gente, che dovresti esser devota,
e lasciar seder Cesar in la sella,
se bene intendi ciò che Dio ti nota. (ll. 82–93 passim)

(And now in thee thy living abide not without war, and
one doth rend the other, of those that one wall and one
foss shuts in.... Ah people, that shouldst be obedient,
and let Caesar sit in the saddle, if well thou understandest
what God writeth to thee!)

The bishop is not only foretelling the course of Shakespeare's history plays, but he is uttering one of the important
articles in the Elizabethan social and political creed; however he does not prevent the lords from making Bolingbroke
king.

One can find (as we have seen) various formulations of
the king as figure of God in *Richard II*. In Dante, Christ is
the ultimate fulfillment of that figure, and probably in
Shakespeare too. But Christ has many meanings which are
relevant in different contexts. In the first part of the play
Richard tends to see himself as a figure of divine power and
majesty, and that is the image he tries to assert in the passage
at Flint Castle which I quoted above. In the abdication scene
he compares his plight, several times, with Christ's. By the
time we meet him in prison (act 5, scene 5) he has learned
to understand the role he played as king, not as men saw
it or should have seen it, but as he actually performed it.
He is meditating on his loneliness and frustration when he
hears music played badly, and it gives him this sad insight:

Ha—ha—keep time! How sour sweet music is
When time is broke, and no proportion kept.
So is it in the music of men's lives.
And here have I the daintiness of ear
To check time broke in a disordered string;
But for the concord of my state and time
Had not an ear to bear my true time broke.
I wasted time, and now doth time waste me.

In this passage music (as frequently in Shakespeare) is an image of harmony in human affairs, corresponding to the garden we noticed in the scene between the queen and the old gardener. It represents both Richard and his country, for he sees that as "God's deputy" he has failed: instead of redeeming the time by harmonizing men's motives with his, he has neglected that great duty and reduced his time to a meaningless succession of minutes: "For now hath time made me his numbering clock."

This monologue sums up, in its concentrated style, the Shakespearian vision of the king as the center of society. It is appropriate that Exton should come at once to murder Richard, and so end both his drama and the "time" in England which he, as king, had created. But *Richard II* must also serve as the first act of the Tudor epic, and Shakespeare uses its final scene to show us Bolingbroke as Henry IV banishing Exton for regicide, and setting the remorseful tone of his own regime:

> The guilt of conscience take thou for thy labour,
> But neither my good word nor princely favor;
> With Cain go wander through shades of night,
> And never show thy head by day nor light.
>
> . . . .
>
> I'll make a voyage to the Holy Land,
> To wash this blood off my guilty hand.

The next play, *Henry IV*, part 1, starts with another reference to Henry's intention of leading a crusade—to make up, no doubt, for his sacrireligious usurpation of the crown. In both plays named for him he continues to feel somehow less than the true king, and his crime will not be fully expiated until long after his death, when Henry VII ends the prolonged civil war by defeating Richard III. Shakespeare's audience would have known very well the happy end of this long sequence of their history, and so might have taken *Richard II* as a tragedy, but one qualified by the Providence of God, which never lost sight of the right rule for England.

King Lear: The Most Comprehensive Version of the Monarchical Theme

King Lear is built on the same principles as *Richard II*, but it is separated from the familiar events of recent history, as well as from the Christian religion which explicitly sustained all the other monarchies that Shakespeare pictured. Lear, like Richard, is the center of his play. His irresponsible gesture of dividing his kingdom starts the sequence of his tragedy, as Richard's failure to settle the Bolingbroke-Mowbray dispute with justice starts his. In both plays the king is the central symbol of order in his society; but when Lear goes wrong far greater chaos results: not only in the community but in the family and in all the individuals of the play. Shakespeare is seeing more deeply into the king figure as the basis of order. Lear is not only king, but he is literal as well as ceremonious sire, and the analogous story of Gloucester and his sons, which Shakespeare combined with the Lear story, throws light on that aspect of the theme.

Shakespeare manages to indicate in the order of Lear's godless Britain the same values he shows in his Christian monarchies. King Lear has as much religious significance in his society as Richard does in his, but neither he nor most of his subjects really understands that. Richard is taken as a *figure* of God, but Lear can hardly be taken that way when most of his subjects have no God. Only Edgar, Cordelia and Albany—and, in a sense, Kent—have enough religion to see the religious order of Britain as a *figure* of the truth; and their religion is very generalized, a matter of "the gods" and not the carefully defined Christian God. Nevertheless we are gradually shown that these three, with their faith, have the truth, and can inherit England when Lear and his tormented time are gone. By the religious actions of these three Shakespeare reveals the meaning of Lear and of his tragedy.

The godless citizens of Lear's kingdom regard it, religiously ordered as it is, with little more than literal vision. The terrible Goneril and Regan have the habit (when the play opens) of treating their father with the cynical-ceremonious respect due to the old king-sire, but what they actually see in him is a feeble old animal best got out of the way. Cornwall agrees with them, and with Lear's daughters he embarks on the quest for absolute power which leads through lust to death. Edmund is their natural ally, seeing the world much as they do; but like Iago he is endowed with wit, energy, and the intelligence to erect his rationalistic morality into an up-to-date philosophy: "Thou nature art my goddess," as he puts it. Old Gloucester believes implicitly in the omnipotence of "the times" themselves, like a gloomy modern victim of *Historismus.* "We have seen the best of our time," he tells us, in many ways; and for him the degeneration of Lear's kingdom and family, like his own troubles with his sons, is simply in the cards at that moment of history. Kent's literal minded faith is in Lear himself, "the body of the king." He cannot separate his faith in the king from his faith in the individual Lear, in whose countenance he sees authority as a dog does in his master's, and when Lear dies he must follow.

These characters have various types of heretical renaissance philosophy; Shakespeare must have met them all in his time. Together they make a most impressive picture of chaos, actual and future. But Shakespeare places it all in relation to the old classical-Christian orthodoxy by means of his three characters who live through it with their insights clear at each stage of the tragic sequence: Edgar, Cordelia, and Albany. It is Edgar who provides the most important clues to the meaning of the drama and eventually shows how its evil time may be redeemed. He begins (when he learns that his father is determined, on false information, to kill him) by realizing that his actual being as son and as citizen is gone: "Edgar I nothing am." He discards the clothes that mean his status in society, and he disappears. His condition then is analogous to Lear's, whose daughters have destroyed his public being as king and as father; and Edgar becomes the most sympathetic and understanding witness of Lear's agony on the heath and in the hovel. In act 4 he meets his blinded father on the way to Dover, and he tries to help the old man by offering him faith instead of fatalism: "Bear free and patient thoughts," he tells him. And when the old man thinks he has fallen over the cliff he accounts for his survival as follows: "Think that the clearest gods, that make them honors of men's impossibilities, have preserved thee." He joins Albany after the final battle and with his permission ceremoniously fights his brother in an "ordeal" which reveals God's will when he is victorious. His role throughout the play follows the Christian pattern of "dying to live," but it is never labeled as Christian. At the very end of the play, when Lear dies, he says: "The weight of this sad time we must obey, speak what we feel, not what we ought to say." That sums up his faith in the most general terms, a faith that God speaks through the events of time. A few years later Shakespeare will make Pericles prince of Tyre think of time and faith in a similar way when he sees the king who reminds him of his father:

> I see that time's the king of men,
> He's both their parent and he is their grave,
> And gives them what he wants, not what they crave. (2.3)

When Shakespeare wrote *Lear* he chose, perhaps out of respect for the setting in pre-Christian Britain, to eliminate all Christian references. But the moral-religious framework is basically the same as that of *Richard II*, the other history plays, and *Hamlet* and *Macbeth*. Lear's monarchy symbolizes all the related values of Shakespeare's traditional society, much as Virgil in the *Purgatorio* sums up the philosophical, ethical-political culture of the classical world as Dante understood it. When at the beginning of the play Lear destroys his monarchy he opens the way to chaos. When at the end the monarchy is restored thanks to Edgar's and Albany's faith, we can see the evil of Lear's time which accounts for the horrifying events we have just been through. During the course of the action our attention was focused on the immediate motives of the characters—the "moral meaning"—but at the end, when faith has been answered, we can see the belief which underlies it all, the "allegorical meaning," *quid credas*.

I wanted to look briefly at *Lear* in order to show that Shakespeare could handle the monarch as *figura* without explicit Christianity. That is because he could assume the actual monarchy of his own time, which embodies the traditional order: he must have been sure that his audience, after the long series of his history plays, would understand Lear's "pre-Christian Britain" by analogy with the monarchy in their own London. It was the existence of that monarchy that enables Shakespeare to use the great medieval or Elizabethan world picture to frame all his serious plays on the real stage.

VI

The Faith in Romantic Love
Dante's Beatrice and Shakespeare's Comedies and *The Winter's Tale*

THE life-giving action of romantic love in Dante and Shakespeare depends on faith, and it is therefore harder to define or represent than the literal fixation on one object which we looked at in Paolo and Francesca and Romeo and Juliet; and it is of course much harder than rational motivation also. It governs the basic orientation of the psyche, like literal romantic love; but because the lover has faith in it, and continually seeks its meaning, it appears differently in different circumstances; and it ideally leads to wisdom.

Dante's Beatrice in the *Inferno* and the *Purgatorio* is the classic image of romantic love: always changing in appearance, yet always representing the object of Dante's faith. When Virgil first mentions her at the beginning of the *Inferno* she is in herself hardly more than a beautiful and pitying lady. The moment we get involved in the infernal scenes we forget her—she is mentioned by name only twice in the whole *Inferno*—yet faith in her necessarily underlies the whole hellish journey. In the *Purgatorio* she is mentioned by name seventeen times, most frequently from canto 15 onward, as Dante absorbs Virgil's rational account of human motivation and begins to seek the faith behind it all. From canto 27 to the end of the poem he imagines, then actually sees, Beatrice, in several contrasting ways. When Virgil with his reason disappears (in canto 30), Beatrice looks like a figure of Christ, *the* object of faith. We may realize that she has, from the first, played the role for Dante of *quid credas* ("what you must believe"); but her relation to Christ is the clearest indication so far of her meaning.

In view of Beatrice's role in the *Inferno* and *Purgatorio*, and her much more important role in the *Paradiso*, are we justified in regarding her as *the* romantic figure? I think we are, for Dante loved her romantically from her first appearance in the *Vita Nuova:* as a mystery demanding that he "hazard all" for her sake. He has simply analyzed the meanings of this love, pushing his analysis of such concrete details as her eyes, or her smile, to their ultimate meaning in his classical-Christian cosmos.

In Shakespeare's comedies, needless to say, we do not find a figure with the scope of Dante's Beatrice. His scene is limited to this world, his characters to such *gentili* young as may be found there. But he too shows romantic love as faith: as demanding total commitment, as changing its appearance, and as leading, at the end of the play, to a perception of earthly peace corresponding to Dante's *Paradiso Terrestre.* He does not, like Dante, go on to Paradise; but he shows the romantic faith as one of the two guides of mankind, the other being the faith in the right king. I have pointed out the parallels between these two faiths of Shakespeare in his second period and the two main motivations of the *Purgatorio*, that represented by Virgil and that represented by Beatrice.

Shakespeare presents his pictures of romantic love as comedies, not only by virtue of their happy endings (in which he is like Dante) but because of the humor with which he sees all his characters. But he never loses sight of the ultimate meaning of his delicate play, and that is why it is illuminating to compare his comedies with Dante's Beatrice, whose meaning, far-reaching and many-sided as it is, is made as explicit as may be.

Dante's Beatrice

It would be essential to study the *Vita Nuova* in detail if one were trying to compare Dante's whole view of romance with Shakespeare's, for that little book is an account of the young Dante's first efforts to understand his love of Beatrice, and so it corresponds to Shakespeare's romantic comedies, which are also youthful works about youth. It is based on thirty-one lyrics of Dante's, which he collects, arranges, and connects with a prose narrative. I have already discussed the first poem, the sonnet which records his frightening dream of Beatrice. The following poems emerge from this love in later circumstances, and the prose narrative recounts the changing relations between Dante, Beatrice, and other friends, from which the poems come.

The *Vita Nuova* is a much subtler and more elaborate little work than I have indicated here, but it is all conceived in the conventions of *amor cortese*, and the concepts of medieval psychology, and it is therefore very difficult for the modern reader. Partly for that reason I do not consider it further, but instead turn to the handling of Beatrice in the *Purgatorio*. When Dante planned this final version of the role of Beatrice he was more than ten years older than he was when he wrote the *Vita Nuova;* Beatrice had died long before; and he had spent years in exile, studying classic philosophy and working out his secular views of politics, philosophy, art, and love. Beatrice was for him a memory, as well as the heavenly vision that he represents. He is able to dramatize her return to him, and thereby his whole relation to her, as it had developed from his earliest youth to the end of his career. His thought and his art were by then both completely mature.

We first hear of Beatrice at the beginning of the *Inferno*. Dante is overcome by terror when he thinks of the journey through Hell which he is supposed to take, and Virgil, to reassure him, tells how Beatrice had appeared to him. She had been sent, it appears, by Lucia and the Virgin Mary to get Virgil's aid for Dante. Dante himself does not meet her here; he only hears about her from Virgil; but what Virgil says is enough to give him the faith he had lost:

Quali fioretti dal notturno gelo
   chinati e chiusi, poi che 'l sol li'mbianca,
   si drizzan tutti aperti in loro stelo:
tal mi fec' io, di mia virtude stanca.   (2.127–130)

(As flowerets, by the nightly chillness bended down and closed, erect themselves all open on their stems when the sun whitens them: Thus I did, with my fainting courage.)

What he gets here is only the fact that Beatrice had moved Virgil and was herself moved by divine grace; he does not get any direct impression of her. She is not mentioned by name again for the remainder of the *Inferno*, but we must assume that Dante's faith in her, dark as it is and unexplored, continues to sustain him as he meets the phantasmagoria of the infernal regions.

When Dante at last reaches the more open scene of the *Purgatorio* Beatrice seems nearer, for Virgil refers to her from time to time as the ultimate authority when Dante questions him on ethics. When Virgil completes his great explanation of human action in canto 18 he refers to her again in this way, and this canto marks the climax of Virgil's guidance. During the third day in purgatory Virgil is an honored companion rather than a guide; and Dante, driven by his "new thirst," is gradually substituting faith for the classical reason with which he had followed Virgil.

The gradual appearance of faith during the third day is important, for it separates Dante from Virgil and finally puts him in touch with Beatrice. Dante thought of faith as involving the whole being, not only the mind, and he indicates that by changing the dominant imagery in cantos 19–27. The imagery in cantos 15–17 is chiefly that of light and dark, which makes visible Dante's intellectual efforts. But when Dante falls into a troubled sleep, and eventually (canto 19) dreams of the siren, the imagery changes, suggesting more bodily things and indicating an awareness "deeper" in the body. We are made aware of those who repent too much attachment to the good things of earth, money, food and drink, sex. We see the avaricious clinging to the ground, the gluttonous fattening and thinning, the lustful in their flames.

By canto 25 Dante (and, one hopes, the reader) is prepared to follow Statius' account of the Christianized Aristotelian doctrine of the soul as the form of the *body*.

Statius' account of the development in the womb resembles modern notions of foetal development; but its importance here is that it presents the soul and body as one. Virgil would agree with that; but in cantos 15–18 he stresses the intellectual and moral powers as all humans possess them, while Statius' explanation looks more closely at the individual, the unique creature with a "new spirit" breathed in by God Himself. Statius agrees with the Thomistic doctrine that it is the bodily substance which accounts for individual variety. So Statius helps Dante to understand the countless unique individuals that he has met beyond the grave, and at the same time Statius prepares him to accept responsibility for his own unique being.

Statius's Aristotelian-Christian account is part of the slow appearance, during the third day of the purgatorial climb, of the many-sided Christian view of humanity. But Dante himself does not at this point actually have the full Christian faith, though he is driven by a need, or "thirst" for it, as he tells us in canto 21:

> La sete natural che mai non sazia
> se non con l'acqua onde la femminetta
> Samaritana domandò la grazia,
> mi travalgiava.   (ll. 1–4)

> (The natural thirst which never is sated, except with the water whereof the poor Samaritan woman asked the grace, was burning within me.)

As he climbs faster and faster, wishing in vain to satisfy his thirst with the good things of earth, or with the intellectual pleasures of his conversation with Statius and Virgil, we learn to see this thirst as a moving force deep in his being. It will eventually lead him to the pageant of Revelation in the *Paradiso Terrestre* (canto 29) which represents the literal object of Christian faith; but by that time we are ready to see that for him it is Beatrice who is the *first* object of the faith that he finds to satisfy his insatiable thirst. Beatrice is for him a "figure" of Christ, and an answer to the same eternally human, natural, but insatiable thirst.

Canto 27 shows the end of the purgatorial climb, where everyone who would continue to the *Paradiso Terrestre* must cross the last wall of fire. Dante must cross it too; it is the first time in the whole journey when he is called upon to risk himself consciously. Below the fire is the guidance of Virgil; beyond it, he is assured, is Beatrice, and the crossing dramatizes the crucial shift from faith in Virgil's reason to faith in Beatrice.

The canto begins with a reference to Christ's blood, which is red like the sunset; Christ is near our consciousness through most of the third day. But the focus in this canto suddenly shifts from the cosmos down to Dante himself, trembling on the edge of the flames, hearing the guardian angel tell them that they must cross: "Wherefore I became, when I heard him," we are told, "such as one who is laid in the grave." Everything is up to Dante himself; what will suffice to get him into the fire? Virgil first tries to persuade him to venture in by assuring him that the flames will not damage him, reminding him of their long association when he had saved him several times. When that fails he asks him to test the flame with the edge of his cloak, but that fails too, and Virgil says, "Now look, my son, between

Beatrice and you is this wall." That, at last, has the desired effect:

> Come al nome di Tisbe aperse il ciglio
>   Piramo in su la morte, e riguardolla,
>   allor che 'l gelso diventò vermiglio:
> così, la mia durezza fatta solla,
>   mi volsi al savio duca, udendo il nome
>   che ne la mente sempre mi rampolla.   (27.37–42)

(As at Thisbe's name Pyramus opened his eyes at the point of death, and gazed at her, when the mulberry became red, so, my stubbornness being softened, I turned me to my wise leader, hearing the name which ever springs up in my mind.)

Virgil smiles, "as one does to a child that is won by an apple," and leads Dante into the flames, talking only of Beatrice, and saying: "Her eyes I seem to see already."

The association with Pyramus and Thisbe shows clearly how Dante's faith in Beatrice would appear to him then. He sees Beatrice as Pyramus sees Thisbe: literally and impatiently; so Paolo and Romeo saw their ladies. When Pyramus jumps to the conclusion that Thisbe has been annihilated by death he sheds his own blood, and so when she appears he is already dying. His love, like Dante's here, is a very youthful love, and Virgil brings that out by comparing Dante to a child who loves an apple. That is the only way in which "love as faith"—even when the faith is in Christ—could appear to Virgil's classical intellect. He sees it as the product of the "natural thirst insatiable in nature," and thus as irrationally demanding the irrational. And he knows that Beatrice herself is quite different from what Dante here imagines. He does not really understand what moves Dante, but he accepts its necessity here.

Having crossed the wall of fire the travelers have only a short way to go before night makes them pause, and they sleep on the edge of the *Paradiso Terrestre*. Dante will meet Beatrice the next morning in the middle of the garden, and he will there undergo an intense series of contradictory impressions; but meantime he sees three female figures, each of whom tells us something about his faith in love: Leah and Rachel when he dreams, and Matelda when he wakes and enters the garden.

Dante's dream of Leah and Rachel corresponds so closely to Matelda and Beatrice, whom he will see next day, that it is almost a daydream of the truth, with little break from his waking consciousness. Leah, according to the biblical interpretation of the time, represents piety of the active type; and her pleasure is to gather flowers, as Dante will see Matelda doing. Rachel represents the higher piety of the contemplative, and finds her satisfaction in gazing into her mirror; she corresponds to Beatrice. When Dante wakes and enters the garden he sees Matelda. He has been told by Virgil that he is now his own king and bishop, and that it is right for him to take his immediate feelings for guide. When he sees Matelda's freedom and beauty he wants to cross the stream and embrace her, but the stream prevents that, and his love for her is held at the elementary level of his first arcadian impression. Matelda moves unthinkingly in perfect obedience to the beauty of the *Paradiso Terrestre*, which had been created directly by God; and Dante, as he follows her, is also obliged to obey all he meets, though it is all beyond his contemplative understanding.

Matelda has been much studied by Dantisti, for she is

a mysterious figure. Her unique action is clearly indicated
in canto 33:

> Come anima gentil che non fa scusa,
>   ma fa sua voglia de la voglia altrui,
>   tosto che è per segno fuor dischiusa.   (ll. 130–132)

> (As a gentle soul that maketh no excuse, but makes her
> will of the will of another, as soon as it is by outward sign
> disclosed.)

The *Paradiso Terrestre* is the outward sign of God's will,
and Matelda obeys it absolutely. She is the spirit of the
original *Paradiso Terrestre*—the biblical prelapsarian Eden,
the classical Golden Age—and is thus the visible form of
Dante's love, just after Virgil tells him to obey himself. She
corresponds to Francesca who makes visible his love just
as he enters Hell. How then is one to understand Matelda's
relation to Beatrice?

When Dante first sees Matelda he has just been initiated
by Virgil into the pre-Christian classical freedom, and as
he enters the *Paradiso Terrestre* that garden looks to him
like Eden before Adam's fall, or the Golden Age of an-
tiquity. He acts with Matelda as though he had Adam's innocence; where he is then, on the earthly side of Lethe,
everything seems to fit the perennial human daydream. It
was of course Dante's faith in Beatrice, as well as Virgil's
guidance, that enabled him to reach this moment of happiness; but it represents only his first impression of his goal,
and it lasts only a moment. For he sees, across Lethe, the
procession of Revelation, filling the garden with supernatural light, and thereby bringing us closer to Eden, not
as it was supposed to have been originally, before the Fall
and the Redemption, but as it is now. The pageant will bring

Beatrice herself, and she, of course, will eclipse Matelda. I think therefore that Matelda represents the "Beatrice" that Dante would have loved and dreamed of—alive, willing, free—if he had been born in Virgil's pre-Christian time. But Matelda proves inaccessible to the real Dante, and he is able to see her only for the one morning that he spends in the *Paradiso Terrestre*.

The pageant of historic Revelation, interrupting the timeless dream of Eden, serves both as the *terminus ad quem* of Dante's purgatorial climb, and also as the *terminus a quo*, for it dimly foretells the *Paradiso* which is still to come. With the rest of the *Paradiso Terrestre* it constitutes the second great turning-point of the *Commedia*, corresponding to the last three cantos of the *Inferno*. It is filled with the ancient symbols of Dante's tradition, and it has been interpreted for us by generations of learned commentators; I make no attempt to analyze it here. But it is essential to consider Dante's meeting with Beatrice, which sums up the whole course of his love up to this point on the edge of paradise.

Dante and Virgil see the historic procession from the earthly side of Lethe, and they can only marvel helplessly. First come seven candelabra, the gifts of the Holy Spirit, which bathe the scene in supernatural light; behind them stream in the air, to a great distance, seven rainbow-colored pennants. Twenty-four elders representing the books of the Old Testament come first; then the four beasts representing the four evangelists; then the car of the church, like a Roman triumphal car, drawn by a griffin, Christ. The car is attended by seven angelic figures, representing the four cardinal and the three theological virtues; and it is followed by twenty-four more elders, representing the final books of the New Testament. The procession stops when the car has reached a point across the river from Dante, and one of the elders, representing the Song of Songs, cries three times, *Veni, sponsa, de Libano*. Then a great throng of angels rises up to fill the air with flowers, and they call *Benedictus qui venis*—the cry with which Christ was greeted on Palm Sunday—and then *Manibus o date lilia plenis*—which father Anchises says, in Virgil's Hades, in praise of young Marcellus. These invocations are all addressed to Beatrice, but they might be addressed to Christ, and Dante at first fails to realize that Beatrice has come.

Beatrice, dressed in white, green, and flame-color (the colors of the Trinity) appears in the car. Her face is veiled by the cloud of flowers, but Dante is shaken to the depths of his being by the unseen power that comes to him from her. This "ancient love" is very similar to what he had felt on earth, in boyhood, when he first saw Beatrice (as he tells us in *Vita Nuova*): a total attachment to her person. He turns to Virgil as a frightened child turns to his mother, to say in the words with which Virgil's Dido recognizes her total love for Aeneas, "I know the signs of the ancient flame." Beatrice's first impact is therefore all earthly literal love for a real woman, and it is all conveyed in the pagan terms that Virgil used to convey Dido's "love that leads to death" (we should remember seeing Dido herself in the lost throng with Paolo and Francesca). But this effect is broken at once when Dante finds that Virgil has disappeared, and Beatrice cruelly interrupts his grief by speaking to him directly:

> "Dante, perché Virgilio se ne vada,
>   non pianger anco, non piangere ancora;
>   ché pianger ti conven per altra spada." (30.55–57)

(Dante, because Virgil leaves thee weep not, weep not yet, for thou must weep for another sword.)

It is here that Dante's acceptance of himself as the individual he really was, which had been growing during the third day's climb, reaches its climax. It is the only time in the *Commedia* that Dante's name is mentioned; and he will be obliged for the rest of canto 30, and until line 90 of canto 31, to contemplate his own literal infidelities, placing them neither in Virgil's moral scheme, nor, as yet, in Beatrice's mercy.

This scene with Beatrice has more of Dante's personal suffering than any other part of the *Commedia*. Beatrice reminds him how he had betrayed his faith in her when she died, and the evidence of his own treachery freezes his heart as the treacherous are frozen in Cocytus, so that their tears are hardened before they fall, depriving them of the relief of mourning. He is melted when he hears angelic voices singing the first verses of Psalm 31: "In thee, O Lord, do I put my trust," and then Beatrice explains why she makes him suffer, speaking first to the angelic presences who cannot understand mortal problems, and then to Dante himself. When she died, and he could no longer see her face, he turned to present good things, girls, art, thought, instead of trying to lift his spirits to heaven, where she was. When he at last brings himself to confess the truth of what she says, the effort makes him faint, and Matelda intervenes to dip him in Lethe and wash away all memory of earthly sin. In this scene Beatrice keeps Dante's attention on himself, but we are aware that her attitude is that of the cruel earthly woman betrayed. At the same time she expresses the severest religious conception of faith: Dante should have been inspired by her death to much greater loyalty, instead of trying to satisfy himself with lesser things. This is one of many contexts in which religious faith in the next world is closely analogous to romantic faith, which also demands "all."

When Matelda has led Dante across the stream of Lethe, and he has forgotten everything wicked he knew on earth, including his own faithlessness, he has left behind the classical pre-Christian Eden which had been ended by Adam's fall, and entered the part of the *Paradiso Terrestre* which represents Eden after Redemption. He is now able to see Beatrice not as the angry earthly woman he had betrayed but as the spirit that is saving him. In her eyes, as she gazes at the griffin, he miraculously sees reflected Christ and his two natures; then, in her mouth, when she reveals it to him, he sees her beauty completed. This is the moment he has been wishing to reach since Virgil told him, at the entrance to Hell, that he would be led to Beatrice. But though he *sees* Beatrice—the literal object of his faith—he does not understand her; nor does he understand any of the things he so clearly sees in the *Paradiso Terrestre*.

For the rest of the *Purgatorio*, cantos 32 and 33, Beatrice leads Dante through the woods and shows him a marvelous series of dreamlike visions of the fate of Revelation, the church, and the empire, for the last thirteen hundred years. Dante fails to understand them too, though they are all so clear visually; and at last Beatrice tells him how he is to react to what he has seen there:

> "Ma, perch'io veggio te ne lo 'ntelletto
> fatto di pietra ed, impietrato, tinto
> sì che t'abbaglia il lume del mio detto,

voglio anco, e se non scritto, almen dipinto,
   che 'l te ne porti dentro a te, per quello
   che si reca il bordon di palma cinto."   (33.73–78)

("But because I see thy mind turned to stone and, stone-
like, such in hue that the light of my word dazes thee, I
also wish that thou bear it away within thee, and if not
written at least painted, for the reason that the pilgrim's
staff is brought back wreathed with palm.")

If one thinks over the *Paradiso Terrestre* since canto 27, one
realizes that Dante the author has done just what Beatrice
advises: he has "painted" the dreamlike sequence of visions
without trying to understand them, and he now offers them
as evidence of his journey as the pilgrims to the Holy Land
offer their palm fronds.

Beatrice is, for Dante, the answer to that "thirst" which
is first mentioned in canto 31, line 1, after Virgil's philosophy has all been expounded. It drives Dante the rest of the
way up the mountain, past the deceptive good things of
earth, and finally past his passionate impressions of Beatrice as the earthly woman he loved. It finally enables him
to see Beatrice as the spirit who reveals to him, when he
looks in her eyes, the paradoxical double nature of Christ,
both divine and human. Beatrice is thus first of all a real
woman and then, gradually, the bearer of her tremendous
meanings—in short—a *figura* of Christ. The heroines of
Shakespeare's comedies are conceived analogously, real
women who mean felicity to their lovers.

Some of Shakespeare's Comedies

By the time Dante reaches the top of the Mount of Purgatory
he has spent his effort on the upward climb; the trope (or

moral meaning) of his journey is clear; and he is ready to accept with faith the visions of the allegory. The characters in Shakespeare's comedies are also without rational moral motives: the plays are all set in dream, in playful entertainment, in magic woods or in the holiday of Twelfth Night. They all trace the love that comes quite early and inspires the faith of the protagonists.

I begin with *The Merchant of Venice*, one of the very earliest, because the analogies between the Portia-Bassanio story and that of Dante's Beatrice are easy to see. Portia lives in Belmont—"beautiful mountain"—which is as far above the merchant's Rialto as the top of the Mount of Purgatory is above the Inferno. She descends to the Rialto to rescue her lover as Beatrice descends to Hell to rescue Dante. The Rialto in fact, like Iago's Venice and Timon's Athens, is a kind of Hell, where money, literal gold, is the chief if not the sole publicly perceptible value. Portia's rescue of Bassanio, which she accomplishes in the great courtroom scene of act 4, consists in revealing first what rational justice says, as Beatrice's emissary Virgil reveals the structure of classical justice in *Purgatorio* 15–18 (the trope), and then the wider perspective of the mercy of God, as Beatrice replaces Virgil's vision after the procession of Revelation (the allegoria). By these revelations she is able to lead the faithful Bassanio out of the commercial torment where "the good of the intellect is lost" to the top of her own beautiful mountain, where images of Eden and the Golden Age prevail.

This allegorical scheme underlies the whole play more completely than I have the space to show. It is, for instance, laconically indicated in the three caskets that Portia's suitors have to choose from, thereby showing what love means to them. The first one, shiny gold, labeled "what many men desire," contains a skull: an obvious example of "the letter that killeth." The silver casket, whose inscription promises what the chooser deserves, interprets its literal appearance tropologically, in terms of rational justice; and it proves to contain the portrait of "a blinking idiot." Shakespeare very often makes fun of those who rely on their own rationalized codes of conduct, especially in the romantic comedies, for the love he is talking about is not a matter of any justice our reason can see: Dante painfully discovers the same thing when Beatrice's appearance makes Virgil disappear. The inscription on the third casket, which is of lead, promises nothing, but it bids the suitor "give and hazard all." That, as I mentioned above, is the rule in all romantic love, fortunate or star-crossed; but if this casket were to represent the death-oriented version of romance it would have to wear the lady's portrait outside, to indicate a response which is not only total but also literal. The leaden outside and the forbidding inscription force the suitor to consult his own motive very soberly; to realize that he doesn't really know what he is doing; and then, if he has the courage, to act in the darkness of hope and faith. But notice that when the casket is opened the delights of the "letter" are all restored: Bassanio finds Portia herself, that *bella persona;* the golden net of her hair, and the gold that enables her to afford to live in Belmont instead of grubbing away in town. Portia's wealth and beauty bring out the unfairness, even the cruelty, of love, a gift which has little or nothing to do with moral desserts as we understand them.

The caskets are a good example of iconography as Shakespeare and Dante use it. Perhaps Shakespeare was

pleased with their ingenuity, like a modern educator playing about with a multiple-choice examination; but he does
not take them seriously in themselves. Their effective meaning must be read in Portia's action as she watches the
guessing game on which she too has been obliged to hazard
all, even herself; in the suitors' efforts to interpret the icons;
and especially in the rest of the play. No sooner has Bassanio
made the right choice than he learns that Antonio, who had
hazarded all for him, has lost. He and Portia (who will
help him) must postpone the enjoyment of their love, hold
it in faith, and, in short, hazard everything once more.

The understanding of love demanded by the third casket
is that of love as faith, and it turns out to be the most concrete of the three. The chooser of gold reacts to that casket
with no more understanding than would be required to
choose any golden object. The chooser of silver considers
his own rationalizations rather than the actual situation
between two individual people. But Bassanio, hesitating before the casket of lead, has to examine his own motive, un-
certain though it appears in value and in outcome, and his
reward is the discovery of the real being, Portia herself.
This realistic orientation upon the actual individual is characteristic of the allegory as distinguished from the trope,
which has to do with the timeless truths of reason. Portia,
like Beatrice, represents *quid credas* for her lover; she too
serves as a figure of Christ.

Where did Shakespeare get the allegorical framework of
The Merchant of Venice which makes it so closely resemble
the Beatrice theme in the *Commedia?* No one knows: it is
not to be found in any of the works usually regarded as his
sources for the play. Portia's dwelling-place in Belmont,

high above the Rialto; the allegory of the caskets; the analogous allegory of Portia's work in the courtroom scene; and
the edenesque symbols of the final return to Belmont—in
short the whole setting and motivation of the play—must
have been devised directly by Shakespeare, on the basis of
the traditional wisdom of love that he shared with Dante.

The other comedies are quite different from each other
and from *The Merchant of Venice* in setting, style, and
mood; but if one looks at their actions one can see that
Shakespeare devised similar forms and meanings for them
all. The young people at the center of each play all have
some version of the same main action: "to find, or secure,
true love." That is the action which he imitates in all his
romantic comedies. And to show this action he bases the
plot, in each play, on mistaken identity, which enables him
to play with disguises, masquerades, and deliberate decep-
tions, as well as the deluded dreams of youthful passion. The
young lovers then pursue their true love through a series of
bewildering appearances, holding on by faith, much as
Dante does at the top of the Mount of Purgatory when he
is at last approaching Beatrice. But Shakespeare's eye is always on *this* life, and he handles his stories lightly, or playfully, however serious a meaning he may see in them.

It is probable that *Midsummer Night's Dream* is the
closest in time to *The Merchant of Venice;* perhaps it was
written directly after it. It is the lightest of the four, as
though Shakespeare had been trying his scheme on ma-
terials as unlike *The Merchant* as possible. Thus, though
Lysander, Demetrius, Hermia and Helena move into the
midnight woods of Athens in faithful pursuit of true love,
their mistakes and illusions are presented farcically, and a

large proportion of the play is devoted to the playful magic of the fairies. The play does not end, like the other three, with Christian weddings, but with the lovers' joyful night together. Oberon blesses their pleasures in bed:

> Now, until the break of day,
> Through this house each fairy stray,
> To the best bride-bed will we,
> Which by us shall blessed be.
> And the issue, there create,
> Ever shall be fortunate,
> So shall all the couples three
> Ever true in loving be.   (5.1)

There are no signs, in Athens, of Christianity; all is maintained at the level of "natural" faith—though it may well be that Shakespeare saw the faith of his young as the expression of that "natural thirst which is never sated" except by the supernatural.

However that may be, Theseus and Hippolyta, at the beginning of act 5, just after they have sorted out the lovers properly, describe the principles Shakespeare has used in plotting the play:

> *Hippolyta*: 'Tis strange, my Theseus, that these lovers speak of.
> *Theseus*: More strange than true, I never may believe
> These antique fables, nor these fairy toys.
> Lovers and madmen have such seething brains,
> Such shaping fantasies, that apprehend
> More than cool reason comprehends.
>
> .   .   .   .
>
> The poet's eye, in a fine frenzy rolling,
> Doth glance from heaven to earth, from earth to heaven,
> And as imagination bodies forth

The forms of things unknown, the poet's pen
Turns them to shapes, and gives to airy nothing
A local habitation, and a name.   (5.1)

Theseus is of course describing the imaginative texture of
the play that we have been watching, the dreamy mixture
of the love quest with the magic play of the fairies; but behind that he sees the *poet's* imagination, sympathetically
moved by love. He would have understood Dante's definition of his own poem-making:

> io mi son un, che quando
> amor mi spira, noto, ed a quel modo
> che ditta dentro, vo significando.

> (I am one who, when love breathes in me, take note, and
> in that mode which he dictates within, go signifying.)

But Hippolyta points to the soberer work of the poet who
had formed and ordered the products of imagination, by
means of his plot:

> *Hippolyta*: But all the story of the night told over,
> And all their minds transfigured so together,
> More witnesseth than fancy's images,
> And grows to something of great constancy:
> But howsoever, strange and admirable.

Hippolyta suggests not only the plot of *Midsummer Night's
Dream* but the formula Shakespeare was to use in plotting
all of his romantic comedies. His gentle young lovers are
completely in love, quite early in the play; they pursue each
other in faith but without understanding; and they encounter an imaginative series of difficulties, which make
the substance of the comedy. But near the end their minds

are "transfigured," their visions clear, and they find that they have "something of great constancy" which is truer than the dreams and disguises they have just been through —usually the Christian weddings that they have needed all along.

Much Ado is much more realistic in its conventions than *Midsummer Night's Dream*. Shakespeare started with the Claudio-Hero tale, according to which Claudio on the eve of his marriage was deceived into thinking Hero unfaithful, and therefore dramatically renounced her. Shakespeare dispenses with all magic in this play, and he draws a fairly credible picture of Leonato's houseparty for Don Pedro, Benedick, Claudio, and Don John. But he carefully establishes the dreamy atmosphere of young love by plotting the whole play as a series of ceremonies: Leonato's masked ball, Claudio's broken wedding to Hero, and his ritual at her "grave." There are also a number of games based on make-believe: the tricks that Claudio and the duke play on Benedick and the women play on Beatrice, and Don John's careful staging of Hero's unfaithfulness, by which he imposes on Claudio. At Don Leonato's long party everything is play of various kinds, and most of it is make-believe sustained by the faith that the gentle young will find their true loves.

Don John is the only one whose make-believe is sinister, and when he shows Borachio to Claudio, climbing into Hero's window, he prepares the ruin of Claudio's wedding. But Shakespeare makes the wedding seem almost as unreal as the masked ball, and when Claudio passionately denounces Hero, Leonato cries, "Are these things spoken or do I but dream?" And then the friar saves the situation by substituting the masquerade of Hero's death for the masquerade of her wedding:

> For it so falls out,
> That what we have, we prize not to the worth,
> Whiles we enjoy it, but being lacked and lost,
> Why then we rack the value, then we find
> The virtue that possession would not show us
> Whiles it was ours. So will it fare with Claudio.
> When he shall hear she died upon his words,
> Th' idea of her life shall sweetly creep
> Into his study of imagination,
> And every lovely organ of her life
> Shall come apparelled in more precious habit,
> More moving-delicate and full of life,
> Into the eye and prospect of his soul,
> Than when she lived indeed.   (4.1)

He tells Hero, "Come lady, die to live; this wedding-day / Perhaps is but prolonged," and that is the way it works. When Claudio learns how Don John had deceived him he says, "Sweet Hero, now thy image doth appear / In the same semblance that I loved it first," and after his ceremonious visit to her "tomb" he can accept the "dead" Hero from her forgiving father—an effect which is both real and dreamlike.

Benedick finds love similarly. He first sees his Beatrice as "slander"—cruel and unforgiving—but then his friends show her to him as really loving him, and he suddenly sees her as the warm woman she had been all along. Hero, Ursula, and Margaret do the like for Beatrice, and when she sees Benedick as loving her she doffs her scornful mask and meets him humbly. When these two pairs of *fedeli d'amore* are at last led to each other they owe their good fortune not to anything they have rationally *done*, but to their friends' aid, and the faith that obscurely held them through all their mistakes and delusions.

With *As You Like It* Shakespeare made a model romantic comedy as he had learned, by that time, to understand the genre. The two central characters, Rosalind and Orlando, are the perfect *gentili* young people; and by act 1, scene 2 they are already "made of faith and service" for each other. The scene of their courtship is Arden, that glamorous forest corresponding to the woods of Athens and to Leonato's houseparty. They are separated, in the pretty woods, by the circumstances of their exile, especially by Rosalind's thin disguise as Ganymede, long enough to make them suffer for their faith; but at last they are united with song and pageantry suggesting Eden and the Golden Age, like the first part of the *Paradiso Terrestre*. They have done little or nothing to earn their happiness, except to keep their faith; and that is usually the way Shakespeare's lovers get together. He did not believe that conscious moral action could achieve love, and he writes all his romantic comedies as "dramas of pathetic motivation." In this play he shows Celia and Oliver "in the very wrath of love" getting together almost as soon as they see each other, perhaps as a mildly ironic comment on the Rosalind-Orlando affair.

There is the usual cast of characters whose love is not romantic, and whose stories thus contrast with those of the gentle people in this play: the older generation; Touchstone, the jester; Audrey, a country girl; and William, a country fellow. Shakespeare also adds those extremely literary figures—the shepherds Corin and Silvius and the shepherdess Phebe—perhaps to mock the conventions of romance which provide the framework for the play. He was certainly using the romance tradition quite consciously, and he summarizes the romantic action of love as faith in act 5, scene 2:

Phebe: Good shepherd, tell this youth what 'tis to love.
Silvius: It is to be all made of signs and tears,
　　And so am I for Phebe.
Phebe: And I for Ganymede.
Orlando: And I for Rosalind.
Rosalind: And I for no woman.
Silvius: It is to be all made of faith and service,
　　And so am I for Phebe.
Phebe: And I for Ganymede.
Orlando: And I for Rosalind.
Rosalind: And I for no woman.
Silvius: It is to be all made of fantasy,
　　All made of passion, and all made of wishes,
　　All adoration, duty and observance,
　　All humbleness, all patience, and impatience,
　　All purity, all trial, all observance,
　　And so am I for Phebe.
Phebe: And so am I for Ganymede.
Orlando: And so am I for Rosalind.
Rosalind: And so am I for no woman.

These formulae might serve to define the lovers' actions in all of the romantic comedies. They serve in this play to prepare the finale, which is more explicitly worked out than the other finales, but expresses the same kind of joyful mood.

In act 5, scene 4 we see all the lovers assembling to get married, and Jacques has this to say: "There is sure another flood toward, and these couples are coming to the ark. Here comes a pair of very strange beasts." He is of course referring to the august notion of divine mercy and forgiveness, though in a mockingly childish way, like the American primitive painting "The Peaceable Kingdom." The love of the gentle young, at this moment of realization, spreads out to include all people. And when all have arrived Hymen, the Greek god of marriage, appears with music and attendants, and he sings:

> Then is there mirth in heaven,
> When earthly things made even
>   Atone [i.e., "at-one"] together.

Pagan god though he is, he expresses very much the same notion of the meaning of this happy moment as the Anglican prayerbook does of marriage, which is soon to follow: "instituted of God, in the time of man's innocency, signifying unto us the mystical union that is betwixt Christ and his Church." The romantic total commitment of the lovers has led, through strange and laughable ordeals, to this miraculous goal. The at-one-ment of male and female means the at-one-ment of classical and Christian, of God and man, of heaven and earth. That wide harmony may be understood as "innocency"—that of the pagan Golden Age, that of the biblical Eden, and at last the innocence that may be restored by faith in Christ. Shakespeare of course does not analyze his symbols. He uses them simply to produce the "chord of feeling" that he wants at this precise moment in his play.

Twelfth Night is most probably the last romantic comedy that Shakespeare wrote, and in it he refers less to the machinery of romance than he does in *Much Ado* and *As You Like It*. Nevertheless he is imitating a very similar romantic action, and he uses analogous devices to present it. With his wonderful language he makes "Illyria" a dreamy edenic scene, suitable for romantic love: "If music be the food of love, play on," as Orsino says in the very first line of the play. He has, as usual, two pairs of gentle young people, Viola and Duke Orsino, and Olivia and Sebastian. He keeps them apart by their mistakes in vision, for both Orsino and Olivia think Viola, in her page boy's costume, a young man. When Sebastian arrives everything is perforce cleared up. What he says when Olivia (mistaking him for Viola) greets him lovingly indicates the feelings, like the first part of the *Paradiso Terrestre*, with which Shakespeare ends this play:

> What relish is in this? How runs the stream?
> Or I am mad, or else this is a dream.
> Let fancy still my sense in Lethe steep;
> If it be thus to dream, still let me sleep. (4.1)

He might be, like Dante, on the bank of the stream which will soon wash away all his evil memories and prepare him for the final vision of his beloved.

Paradoxes of the Happy Ending: *The Winter's Tale*

The modern reader is likely to mistrust the happy endings of Dante's and Shakespeare's accounts of the course of love as faith. But the two authors were well aware of this difficulty, and one can see, with careful reading, that they so limit and define their moments of happiness as to bring out the brevity and the paradoxical quality of any such human experience. They seem to have been as skeptical of the possibility of prolonged earthly happiness as we are.

Both accept the convention that comedy must end happily. Dante in his letter to Can Grande, explaining why he called his great poem a comedy, writes, "comedy introduces some harsh complication, but brings its matter to a prosperous end," which he did in his poem; and Shakespeare also accepted this convention. But they both had strict notions of what happiness would be, if we had it; and they are both faithful to their experience when they present it. In their works happiness appears as a momentary dream or vision.

Dante in his account of the *Paradiso Terrestre* carefully agrees with the contemporary conception of the reality of Eden. It looks one way if considered as Adam saw it before his fall, and another way after the Fall and the Redemption. Dante's contemporaries believed that man could not live in Eden but could only glimpse it on the way to heaven, and accordingly Dante sees it only briefly on the morning of his fourth day. He sees it, moreover, as the temporary answer to his *sete natural che mai non sazia* (natural thirst which is never satisfied), the literal *figura* of his faith in love: the allegory which will not be explained until the anagoge of the *Paradiso*. Therefore he sees all its visions with extraordinary clarity but with a minimum of understanding. When at the end Beatrice tells him that when he returns to earth he must record all he saw literally (but without trying to understand), the reader can see that she has defined the style in which the *Paradiso Terrestre* has been written. She has also defined the "style" of Dante's action as the pilgrim; at the wonderful moment of the end of the *Purgatorio* author and protagonist coincide in their contact with the mysterious visions of man's earthly goal. This moment is "real," and packed with inexplicit meanings, but brief.

Shakespeare, presenting his happy endings on earth and

in this life, cannot make such extensive use of the fourfold allegory as Dante does in the *Commedia;* but his commedies move by faith, and not the moral will, and so suggest religious or allegorical rather than moral meanings at the end, as the *Paradiso Terrestre* does. When he calls them *Midsummer Night's Dream* or *Much Ado About Nothing* or *As You Like It* or *Twelfth Night, or What You Will*, he indicates the self-indulgent faith in their make-believe with which we must see them, and also the way in which he was inspired to write them. When "love breathed in him" that way he could, by his verbal style alone, make the silliest characters and stories charming and make the happy weddings, with which they all end, the only possible conclusions. It would be easy to regard the romantic comedies as simply the triumph of Shakespeare's style, endorsing Orsino's remark, "If music be the food of love, play on," without inquiring whether he wanted to indicate the relation of his comedies to reality or not. But I think he consciously and habitually used his style to define the paradoxicality, the limited and special reality, of the plays that end happily.

The Winter's Tale is a good place in which to study Shakespeare's conscious use of his comic style, for in that play he notoriously mixes his styles. It was written near the end of his career, and it shows the return of the beloved Hermione to her husband Leontes who had unjustly accused her of adultery and then spent sixteen years of repentance. The return of romantic love in another generation makes the play closer to the *Commedia* than the earlier comedies, and it is probably Shakespeare's maturest version of love as faith.

The play begins in a "realistic" style when Leontes, king

of Sicilia, erroneously decides that Hermione is being unfaithful to him with his old friend Polixenes, king of Bohemia. Both kings remember their boyhood together:

> We were as twinned lambs, that did frisk i'the sun
> And bleat the one at the other. What we changed
> Was innocence for innocence; we knew not
> The doctrine of ill-doing, nor dreamed
> That any did. (1.1)

We have just seen Leontes, Polixenes, and Hermione enjoying each other in similar innocence; but that does not prevent Leontes from falling suddenly into a violent fit of jealousy. He accuses Hermione of adultery and sends her to prison, where she presently gives birth to a daughter. Polixenes has to flee for his life, and Leontes, who believes his daughter was begotten by Polixenes, induces his follower, Antigonus, to take the babe away and leave her to die. He brings Hermione to trial, and at the same time sends to the Oracle of Apollo to learn the truth. At the trial he gets the Oracle's word: "Hermione is chaste, Polixenes blameless, Camillo a true subject, Leontes a jealous tyrant, his innocent babe truly begotten, and the King shall live without an heir, if that which is lost be not found." Leontes at first tries to ignore the oracle, but then he learns that his beloved young son, Mamillius, has just died. Hermione faints, and she is removed by Paulina. These blows open Leontes' eyes, and he is beginning to confess his crimes when Paulina returns to report that Hermione too has died. Leontes resolves to devote the rest of his life to repentance and to mourning his family. This third act (and the first sequence of the play) ends with the "unrealistic" scene of Antigonus "on the seacoast of Bohemia" with the babe. He presently exits, "pursued by a bear," leaving the babe and a treasure, both of which are found by the old shepherd and his son, who rescue the foundling.

There can be no doubt that Shakespeare intended the improbability of this episode—the babe lost on the non-existent "seacoast of Bohemia," and Antigonus devoured by a bear, as we soon learn—to bid the audience accept the rest of the play in the spirit of an old tale, or one of his own early romances. This transition is prepared for only by the episode of the oracle (act 3, scene 1), which is filled with the atmosphere of divinity behind nature and behind the realistic sequence of Leontes' and Hermione's hellish sufferings. It is immediately followed by the appearance of Time as chorus, with his limping old-fashioned couplets, and his attitude of the teller of old tales. The old shepherd hints at what is to follow when he tells his son (who has seen Antigonus' sad fate while the old shepherd found the babe): "Thou mettest with things dying, I with things new-born."

Act 4 is about "things new-born": Leontes' lost daughter Perdita and Polixenes' runaway son Florizel. The style of this whole act is very close to that of the earlier romantic comedies. We meet the two young people at the old shepherd's spring festival, which corresponds to Illyria or the Forest of Arden. They are totally in love, but faithfully so: "Since my desires / Run not before mine honour, nor my lusts / Burn hotter than my faith," as Florizel says. They are separated by their ignorance of Perdita's real identity, for they both think she is really the old shepherd's daughter. When Polixenes and Camillo arrive, disguised, in search of Florizel, the young people's affair is threatened. After

Perdita gives everyone his appropriate flower, she and
Florizel dance with the shepherds and shepherdesses; they,
the marvelous rogue Autolycus, and the dancing satyrs who
soon replace the shepherds correspond to the clowns of the
romantic comedies. But the pretty scene is rudely ended
when Polixenes reveals himself, forbids his son to marry
the pretty "shepherdess," and departs in anger. Perdita
wants to give up her Florizel, but he is inspired all over
again: he assures her that her dignity cannot fail "but by
/ The violation of my faith, and then / Let nature crush the
sides o' the earth together / And mar the seeds within."
Camillo offers to take Florizel and Perdita to Sicilia, and to
try to persuade Leontes to intervene in their favor with
Polixenes; and the whole cast of the pastoral comedy sets
forth for Leontes' court.

The fifth act presents the improbably happy endings
which Florizel's faithful love for Perdita, and Leontes'
much longer faithful love for his Hermione, find at last. It
consists of a carefully plotted series of recognition scenes.
The act opens with Leontes renewing his pledge to Paulina
that he will never betray his wife's memory to marry again.
Then Florizel and Perdita appear, and Leontes recognizes
his old friend's son but does not yet realize who Perdita is.
They are interrupted by a report that Polixenes has forbidden Florizel to marry Perdita, and Leontes agrees to in-
tercede to persuade Polixenes to relent. In scene 2 we see
Autolycus cynically hearing, from three gentlemen, the
news of the joyful meeting between Leontes and Polixenes,
and then of the even more joyful discovery (by means of
Perdita's treasure brought by the old shepherd), that she
is actually Leontes' own daughter, and so admirably suited

to marry Florizel. "This news, which is called true, is so like an old tale that the verity of it is in strong suspicion," says the third gentleman; and presently he reports that Antigonus' death was "like an old tale still." This act gathers all the improbable episodes of the play, from the oracle (act 3, scene 1) through the events of Perdita's life, to bring them to bear on the happy ending.

Scene 3, which shows the meeting between Leontes and Hermione, is the most joyful and the least probable episode of the act. Shakespeare had carefully concealed the fact that Paulina had saved and hidden Hermione when she took her away sixteen years before. Now he has everyone assemble in "a chapel in Paulina's house," ostensibly to see her statue of Hermione. As they gaze at it, it gradually becomes evident that the statue is the living Hermione. She descends, with music, to embrace Leontes. This episode is entirely Shakespeare's invention. In his source, *Pandosto, the Triumph of Time* by Robert Greene, Queen Hermione dies, Leontes commits suicide when his crimes are revealed, and the happy ending consists only in the marriage of Florizel and Perdita. By changing the plot Shakespeare made the Leontes-Hermione story the main romantic theme, and he reduced the Florizel-Perdita episode to daydream like the early comedies. He put their pretty affair in the fourth act, where it is related to the main Leontes-Hermione story as the premonitory dreams and visions of the fourth acts of many other plays of his, especially the tragedies, are related to the main action. Leontes' discovery of his wife thus becomes more important than Florizel's recognition of Perdita (which occurs offstage), and it acquires a solider, realer quality in spite of the fairy-tale device of the living statue.

Perhaps Shakespeare was thinking of the difference between Leontes' sixteen-year vigil and the much lighter troubles that Florizel's faith has to survive. If we make-believe the living statue, our "faith" will be rewarded by the satisfaction—Leontes' appropriate but unexpected rediscovery of his beloved wife—of the "thirst" which has been troubling us throughout the play.

What are we to think of the frankly stressed improbabilities in this play? Shakespeare used them, of course, to make the "old tale" atmosphere that he thought necessary. But in doing so he assumed, like Dante near the top of the Mount of Purgatory, the "natural thirst insatiable in nature"; and, again like Dante, he knew that this common human "thirst" might be interpreted either romantically or religiously. Dante, for his happy ending, offers the griffin, Christ, and also various visions of his beloved Beatrice. Shakespeare offers Hermione; but the whole course of Leontes' life might be read as a parable with the religious meaning of "dying to live." Moreover both authors believed that what we see here on earth is at least partly created by our thirst and our faith: "We are such stuff as dreams are made on," Prospero puts it. By stressing the improbabilities Shakespeare makes it easy for us to "believe" Leontes' story, and by briefly satisfying our feelings and Leontes' he "proves" the only reality he is sure of: the common human need for love as faith.

VII

Belief and Make-Believe
Poetry as Evidence of Things Not Seen

The *Paradiso Terrestre* and *The Tempest*

Dante's *Paradiso Terrestre* (the last six cantos of the *Purgatorio*) is much more explicitly Christian than Shakespeare's *Tempest*. It plainly represents Eden, of course; and when the procession of Revelation enters the forest, with its elders who stand for the books of the Bible, its car drawn by the griffin who means Christ; its nymphs and lights and candelabra of religious significance, there is no doubt that Dante is picturing Christianity as it was visible to him, after he had climbed the Mount of Purgatory under Virgil's guidance. In *The Tempest* there are no references to Christianity, and though it is as religious as the *Paradiso Terrestre* its religion is represented only in the attitudes of the characters, especially Prospero's, and not in any visible symbols of Christian belief. The *Paradiso Terrestre* is the earthly end of Dante's whole journey from the darkness of Hell to his Christian heaven; *The Tempest* is a romance, like Shakespeare's other late plays; and it is presented lightly, as make-believe: we are free to take or to leave its deeper meanings.

In spite of these and many other differences there are important analogies between the two works. Both picture the human psyche after the main struggles of life are over, a contemplative moment on the outer edge of human experience, just before the miraculous flight to heaven in the case of Dante, and in the case of Shakespeare when "every third thought must be my grave," as Prospero puts it. In both works there are old, and final, *reprises* of important themes from the poet's life. In both a young girl who sees life freshly—Matelda in Dante's poem, Miranda in Shakespeare's play—provides the occasion for the whole visionary experience. Dante is himself the central character—almost the *only* one—in the *Paradiso Terrestre;* and Prospero, a figure of Shakespeare, is the most important character in *The Tempest.* The *Paradiso Terrestre* is what Dante sees, and represents for us poetically; and the whole story of *The Tempest* is arranged and made visible by Prospero with the aid of Ariel.

The underlying actions of the two works are similar: "to see one's freedom at last"—"freedom" being understood in several different ways. Virgil gives Dante classical freedom when he makes him king and bishop over himself, on the threshold of Eden; and Dante enters that realm to enjoy it, guided only by his own desires. In *The Tempest* Caliban and Ariel, as well as all the castaways, seek to free themselves from their confinement on the island; and Prospero frees everyone, and thereby himself from his obligations to them, at the end of the play. But this motive is understood in many ways, as I have said; and in both works the paradoxical freedom which is finally attained turns out to coincide with some form of obedience, after images of innocence, guilt, and redemption, and innocence regained, have succeeded each other in several patterns.

In both works the meaning must be understood as "allegory" rather than "trope," for they are concerned with what faith can see here on earth after reason and the moral will have done all they can: the ceiling which the psyche, driven by love—its' "natural thirst insatiable in nature"—can see at the end of its lifelong climb. With that in mind one can more easily understand the wonderful styles of the two works. Visual images, the music of language, and the dreamlike sequences of plot are more important than the realistic conflicts and characterizations that make the violent life of Dante's *Inferno* and *Purgatorio* and of Shakespeare's histories and tragedies. In the tempests of the midst of life the psyche's wrong turnings are painfully sorted out in the light of reason, but in the final phase the overall shape which faith has given the journey seems more significant than the details. As action reaches its end, it takes the form of an effort to *see*—which is accomplished in various ways. Hence the shifting pageantry of the *Paradiso Terrestre* and the masquelike quality of *The Tempest.* Mark Van Doren wrote of *The Tempest:* "Any set of symbols, moved close to this play, lights up as in an electric field."[1] Dante is not supposed to write that way, but the pageantry of the *Paradiso Terrestre*, though made of traditional elements, may also be interpreted in various ways, as the labors of erudite commentators show. Dante's intention seems to have been to leave the mixture of Hebrew, Greek, Latin, and other sources which he used irridescent, at least in its primary effect.

I now wish to compare the poets' actions as they made

their poems. They were always aware of the work of poetry, and often point it out, but in these two terminal pieces they take special care to dramatize themselves engaged in their task. Dante pictures himself directly, and Prospero is a figure of Shakespeare, like the duke in *Measure for Measure*. By watching these two characters one may learn something about the authors' conceptions of poetry and its relation to religious belief.

The Poetry: Lyric and Plot

It is the lyric beauty of *The Tempest* and also of much of the *Paradiso Terrestre* that is most striking at first, and it is the lyricism that primarily attracted Pound and Eliot when they were seeking nourishment for their own poetry. Pound, as he explains in *The Spirit of Romance*, is fascinated by canto 28 of the *Purgatorio*, with its echoes of Dante's early lyricism. Eliot, in *The Waste Land*, quotes Ferdinand's reference to Ariel's song: "This music crept by me upon the waters."[2] Pound and Eliot were recognizing the kind of poetry upon which much of the best modern theory is based: "pure poetry," which may be regarded as an end in itself with no more obvious a relation than that of music to the rest of experience. Dante and Shakespeare had the secret of that magic, but neither thought that it alone constituted the whole venerable art of poetry. In the *Paradiso Terrestre* and *The Tempest* the lyric effects always lead straight to narrative or drama.

Dante's theory of poetry was a theory of inspiration: "I am one who, when love inspires [or breathes in] me, take note, and in that mode which he dictates within go signifying," as he tells Bonagiunta in *Purgatorio* 24. In his youth he understood inspiration almost as a modern poet might, jealously safeguarding its mystery, trying to authenticate his verses by making them obey only the particular voice. But when after Beatrice's death he read Aristotle, he learned to understand that his love for Beatrice was only one mode of the *energeia* that moves all men and all things, and the way was open for a far wider conception of poetry, eventually the full classic notion of the imitation of action in all its modes. Poetry is still a matter of inspiration, a voice the poet must hear within if the poetry is to *be* poetry; but now he knows it is fed from many sources and may speak in many modes besides the lyrical. And the music of the beginning of canto 28 leads us on into the larger form—narrative and dramatic—of which the verbal music is only one aspect.

In *The Tempest* Ariel's songs serve as inductions, but at the same time Shakespeare uses Ariel to show the role of the poet's sensuous imagination in the total creative action. Prospero, as I have said, is a figure of his creator, and Ariel is a figure of the image-making power of the poet. It is through Ariel that Prospero raises the tempest with which the play begins; through Ariel that he charms Ferdinand and us, appalls the treacherous Alonso, Antonio, and Sebastian, leads and soothes Ferdinand and Miranda with his pastoral pageantry—and so on. Ariel acts exactly like the inspired poet's imagination as Theseus describes it in *A Midsummer Night's Dream*, act 5: he makes the important parts of the sensuously perceptible texture of the play. But just as the story of that play, when it is all told over, "more witnesseth than fancy's images," as Hippolyta puts it, so does the story of *The Tempest;* and if we are to understand its poetry we must watch Prospero as he sets up the plot of the whole play.

I have said that in *The Tempest* and the *Paradiso Terrestre* the musical arts of language, and the plot, are the most important elements of the poet's art. Of course characterization and the nonlyrical modes of language are there when needed, but it is the verbal music and the plot that most completely account for the two works. In both "the plot is the soul of the tragedy," as Aristotle put it: the plot makes both the form of the play and its meaning. The meaning is not to be separated out as a thesis, it *is* the sequence of incidents. The poet-plotmaker arranged the incidents as a painter arranges the visible elements on his canvas, or the lyric poet his words and images: to add up to the effect he wants. That is why any good plot produces some of the true tragic effect when merely recounted, without benefit of characterization or poetic language.

Both authors arrange the incidents to show the main stages of their growth in awareness—from initial innocence, through the sufferings and infidelity of maturity, to innocence regained in a new way. Dante enters the garden with the innocence that he has just learned from Virgil; and at once he meets Matelda, who, since she exists entirely in obedience to the beauties of Eden, is herself the very spirit of innocence. The pageant of Revelation then brings Beatrice, and she suddenly wakens Dante's passion, as Aeneas had wakened the lost Dido's. When Dante weeps, discovering that Virgil is gone, Beatrice sternly reproaches him for his infidelity to her, then and ten years earlier. She rehearses his pursuit of various girls, after her death, and his infatuation with classical philosophy in the "dark wood" of his life. When he has confessed with great agony, and been led across Lethe, which removes all memory of evil, he is ready to see the beauty of Beatrice with innocence regained:

> O isplendor di viva luce etterna,
>   chi palido si fece sotto l'ombra
>   sì di Parnaso, o bevve in sua cisterna,
> che non paresse aver la mente ingombra,
>   tentando a render te qual tu paresti
>   là dove armonizzando il ciel t'adombra,
> quando ne l'aere aperto ti solvesti?   (31.139–145)

(O splendour of living light eternal, who has ever grown so pale under Parnassus' shade or drunk so deep of its well that he would not seem to have a mind disabled, trying to render thee as thou appearedst there, heaven with its harmonies overhanging thee, when in the free air thou didst disclose thyself?)

Presently he will be able to tell her:

> "Non mi ricorda
> ch'i' stranïasse me giammai da voi,
> nè honne coscïenza che rimorda."   (33.91–93)

(I have no remembrance that I ever estranged me from you, nor have I conscience of it that pricks me.)

This sequence suggests a simplified version of Dante's own experience and his own writings: the innocence of youth, the passion and the infidelities of his exile when he lost his way, and the new innocence that he gained when his faith in Beatrice returned and he started writing the *Commedia.*

The pattern of *The Tempest* is based upon what Prospero looks at, and shows his audience; and it is clearly analogous to Dante's plot. After the tempest created by Prospero and

Ariel we see Miranda, who corresponds to Matelda, and then Alonso's son Ferdinand. Those two carry the theme of initial innocence, and like Perdita and Florizel in *The Winter's Tale* they symbolize the aim of the older generation. We then see the castaways, Alonso the king of Naples, and Sebastian his brother; Prospero's brother Antonio, who usurped the dukedom of Milan; the good old Gonzalo and other courtiers. Antonio and Alonso had exiled Prospero and his infant daughter years before; their appearance now again replaces Miranda, and while Alonso and Gonzalo sleep Antonio and Sebastian once more stubbornly prepare to attempt usurpation by murdering the other two. Prospero sends Ariel to waken Alonso and Gonzalo in time, and then, after a scene with Caliban, Stephano, and Trinculo—a lighter version of the courtiers' treachery— we see the climax and turning point of the play. The court party is weary after long meandering, and Ariel pretends to serve them a banquet. When they try to eat it he removes it, and then explains their true situation to them:

> But remember,
> For that's my business to you, that you three
> From Milan did supplant good Prospero.

The "powers" are now punishing them:

> Thee of thy son, Alonso,
> They have bereft, and do pronounce by me
> Lingering perdition—worse than any death
> Can be at once—shall step by step attend
> You, and your ways, whose wrath to guard you from—
> Which here, in this most desolate isle, else falls
> Upon your heads—is nothing but heart's sorrow,
> And a clear life ensuing.   (3.3)

After which Antonio and Sebastian depart unrepentant, "to fight the fiends," and Alonso rushes out to join his son who, he thinks, is "mudded" in the ooze. Gonzalo and the other courtiers follow, to save them if they can.

This scene, the climax of the long struggle between Prospero, Alonso, Sebastian, and Antonio, corresponds to the scenes between Dante and Beatrice in cantos 30, 31, and 32. When Beatrice first appears she seems to promise erotic satisfaction, and Ariel at first offers delicious food. Beatrice at once turns into a stern judge, and Ariel's banquet is removed by a harpy. Ariel tells the court party what repentance would require—"heart's sorrow"—and Beatrice imposes the sorrow on Dante. The chief difference between the patterns of the two scenes is that Dante himself realizes the truth of his infidelity, and bitterly repents, while Antonio and Sebastian hear without belief, and Alonso, who thinks his son is drowned, despairs instead of repenting. Prospero's power is mainly that of poetry, which can at the most *show* the truth; and when he has shown the castaways what their situation really is, he has done almost all he can to free himself from his obligations to them. He does not, like Dante in the analogous scene, face himself here; he postpones that until the end of the play when he releases everyone for the return to Naples, and then removes the layers of make-believe which have made him the Prospero that we knew, appearing briefly as the poor player who had made the show.

After this scene innocence can return: Prospero releases Ferdinand from his log-toting, gives Miranda to him, and bestows upon their eyes and ours "some vanity of mine art"—a masque with dance, music, and lyric verse. This is of course an edenic dream; but Prospero, when he remembers that Caliban, Trinculo, and Stephano are coming to murder him, has to interrupt it. When he explains that "we are such stuff as dreams are made on," we may reflect that Ferdinand and Miranda are made, at the moment, of the daydream he offered them; that the courtiers are made of their stubborn dreams of power; and that Caliban's new allies Stephano and Trinculo are made of their dreams of vulgar loot. The time has come to waken everyone and end the play. We can see that Ferdinand and Miranda have an innocence which is still only dreamy. Like Perdita and Florizel in *The Winter's Tale* they represent only the promise of the dreamless innocence their father will reach at the end of the play, when, like Dante after he crosses Lethe, he reaches an innocence of total obedience to the will of God.

T. S. Eliot's *Marina*

T. S. Eliot, when thinking over his career late in life, made frequent use of the innocence-repentance sequences he found in the upper *Purgatorio* and the late Shakespeare plays. The structure of *Marina*, for instance, reflects this sequence. The title of the poem is the name of Pericles' daughter in *Pericles, Prince of Tyre;* but Eliot might have had in mind any of the lost and found daughters in the last four plays of Shakespeare, as well as some of the features of the poetry at the top of the Mount of Purgatory. The poem begins with memories of youth, associated with the "daughter":

> What seas what shores what grey rocks and what islands
> What water lapping the bow
> And scent of pine and the woodthrush singing through the
> fog
> What images return
> O my daughter.

That is interrupted by the sequence on death, which corresponds to the scene where Dante is convicted of faithlessness by Beatrice, and to the scene in *The Tempest* where the castaways are convicted of treachery by Ariel. Eliot writes:

> Those who sharpen the tooth of the dog, meaning
> Death
> Those who glitter with the glory of the humming-bird,
> > meaning
> Death

and the rest. Then these figures

> Are become unsubstantial, reduced by a wind,
> A breath of pine, and the woodsong fog
> By this grace dissolved in place

and the lost innocence and hope of youth return in a kind of *intermittence du coeur:* "Whispers and small laughter between leaves and hurrying feet / Under sleep, where all the waters meet." The poet then accepts that remembered life as the clue to his present existence, when he may be innocent again:

> > let me
> Resign my life for this life, my speech for that unspoken,
> The awakened, lips parted, the hope, the new ships.
>
> > What seas what shores what granite islands towards my
> > > timbers
> And woodthrush calling through the fog
> My daughter.

Marina is of course only a brief lyric, but its plot moves from the innocence of childhood, through the deathly remorse of maturity, to the return of innocence in a new form.

Marina is at least partly derived from Shakespeare and Dante, and the *Paradiso Terrestre* and *The Tempest* are

partly derived from their authors' readings. Dante refers
to many books as he writes: classic poets on the Golden Age,
Virgil's *Aeneid*, the books of the Bible. Prospero tells Miranda (1.2) that Gonzalo provided him, as he went into
exile, with books that he prizes above his dukedom; and
at the end of the play he renounces his books along with
Ariel and his staff to dramatize the ending of his work as
poet. Shakespeare seems still to have conceived his writing
as old Gower described it in *Pericles:* "I tell you what mine
authors say." But neither he nor Dante found their plots
literally in any of their reading. That ur-narrative sequence,
which embodies the meaning of a life lived by faith from
the cradle to the grave, seems to have been derived from
all their reading, writing, and experience, in the light of
their classical-Christian tradition.

Belief and Make-Believe

Neither Dante in the *Paradiso Terrestre* nor Shakespeare
in *The Tempest* is trying to present the ultimate object of
his belief. Shakespeare never considers the mystic vision of
God, and Dante approaches it only in the *Paradiso*, after he
has drunk of Lethe and Eunoe, and been inspired by Beatrice. Dante's Eden and Shakespeare's magic isle are of
course very special places, but both are essentially on the
familiar earth. Dante planned the *Paradiso Terrestre* to
represent the allegorical meaning of his journey—"what
you must believe"—made visible to him after he had absorbed Virgil's moral enlightenment. *The Tempest*, too,
shows the form and meaning that Shakespeare believed he
could see in his life, when he was near its end.

Both poets stage themselves in their poems, and that

enables them to criticize their visions even as they present them. According to their Aristotelian psychology, action has two causes—the needs or desires of the psyche, and what it is able to see. Vision and desire thus affect each other, and it is often hard to decide which is the more important in making what we see. We may often have the impression that the *Paradiso Terrestre* and *The Tempest* show only what their authors wanted to see; but they were well aware of that possibility, and by showing themselves, and continually reminding us of their presence as both seers and poets they take account, in the only possible way, of the limitations inherent in any human vision.

Sometimes they speak out in their own voices as the man who is even then trying to make the poem. Dante breaks his narrative for this purpose when he first sees the Divine Pageant, invoking the classical muses:

> O sacrosante Vergini, se fami,
>   freddi o vigilie mai per voi soffersi,
>   cagion mi sprona ch'io mercé vi chiami.
> Or convien che Elicona per me versi,
>   e Uranìa m'aiuti col suo coro
>   forti cose a pensar mettere in versi.   (29.37–42)

(O most holy virgins, if fastings, cold, or vigils I have ever borne for you, need drives me to ask you for reward; now must Helicon pour forth for me and Urania help me with her choir to put in verse things hard for thought.)

A little later he writes:

> A descriver lor forme più non spargo
>   rime, lettor; ch'altra spesa mi strigne
>   tanto, ch'a questa non posso esser largo;

ma leggi Ezechïel, che li dipigne
come li vide da la fredda parte
venir con vento con nube e con igne.   (ll. 97–102)

(To describe their forms, reader, I do not waste more
rhymes, for other outlay so presses on me that I cannot
be lavish in this; but read Ezekiel, who depicts them as
he saw them come from the cold parts, with wind and
cloud and fire.)

Prospero frankly tells Miranda that he had made the tempest that frightened her:

The direful spectacle of the wreck which touched
The very virtue of compassion in thee,
I have with such provision in mine art
So safely ordered, that there is no soul—
No not so much perdition as an hair
Betid to any creature in the vessel
Which thou heard'st cry, which thou saw'st sink.   (1.2)

Throughout the play we see Prospero making the plot by means of Ariel, who leads the castaways by the sounds and visions he offers them.

Both poets also take part in their poems, especially Dante. He shows with care what his state is at each stage of his exploration, thus partly accounting for what he sees. Virgil prepares him to see Eden by freeing him—crowning and mitring him over himself—and the garden inhabited by Matelda first appears to him as it might have to a classical poet: as the free dream of the Golden Age. When this scene is invaded by the pageant of Revelation Dante is as astonished as Virgil, and can see hardly more than what the eye gives him. When Beatrice first appears he sees her with an earthly man's passion, until she bitterly reproaches him for his infidelity. When he has repented, crossed Lethe, forgotten all evil, and been sustained by the seven virtues, he is able to see her with his innocence restored. She then appears to him in all her beauty, and she shows him the transformations of the tree of the knowledge of good and evil, and the nightmare figures that indicate the destructive relations between the two guides of mankind, the Empire and the Church. All of this he can see, with his newly restored innocence, only literally. Beatrice understands that, and eventually tells him how he must write about what he has seen:

> "Ma perch' io veggio te ne lo 'ntelletto
>   fatto di pietra e, impetrato, tinto
>   sì che t'abbaglia il lume del mio detto,
> voglio anco, e se non scritto, almen dipinto,
>   che 'l te ne porti dentro a te per quello
>   che si reca il bordon di palma cinto."   (33.73–78)

("But since I see thee turned to stone in thy mind, and being petrified, darkened, so that the light of my speech dazzles thee, I will also that thou bear it away within thee, and if not written at least pictured, for the reason that the staff is brought back wreathed with palm.")

Beatrice is thinking of the pilgrims to the Holy Land, who return with palm fronds on their staffs, to prove that they have actually been there. That accurately describes his relation to the *Paradiso Terrestre:* he has seen it all freely but with hardly more than literal understanding, and then obediently recorded it that way. Beatrice thus shows clearly how Dante's changing action accounts for what he has seen and written at this point in his journey.

In *The Tempest* the interplay between action and vision is shown in a different way in each member of the cast—

with the result that we can hardly tell what the island really is. Good old Gonzalo sees it as almost the *Paradiso Terrestre*, ready to be made the goal of rational human government:

> All things in common nature should produce
> Without sweat or endeavor. Treason, felony,
> Sword, pike, knife, gun, or need of any engine,
> Would I not have. But nature should bring forth
> Of its own kind, all foison, all abundance,
> To feed my innocent people. (2.1)

Antonio and Sebastian see it as foul:

> *Adrian:* The air breathes upon us here most sweetly.
> *Sebastian:* As if it had lungs, and rotten ones,
> *Antonio:* Or, as 'twere perfumed by a fen.

Caliban, Ariel, Stephano and Trinculo, and Ferdinand—each sees the isle as the habitual direction of his love enables him to see it. Prospero knows that—"we are such stuff as dreams are made on"—and his attempts to show them something different fail on the whole. When through Ariel he demonstrates to Alonso, Antonio, and Sebastian their actual situation, none of them believes what he sees. The pastoral pageant that he shows Miranda and Ferdinand delights but hardly surprises them. And he offers Stephano and Trinculo the very trumpery he knows their eyes incurably crave. It is even doubtful that he really changes their actions or their visions at the end of the play, when he gradually dispels the make-believe of his isle.

At the ends of their works both authors show themselves as characters coinciding with themselves as authors: the

point at which the work must end. When it is high noon
at the top of the Mount of Purgatory Dante sees a spring
whose waters slowly divide, and he is told that the two
streams it makes are Lethe and Eunoe. Matelda had told
him earlier, but he had completely forgotten. "Perhaps a
greater care, which often robs the memory, has darkened
his mind," says Beatrice (33.24). She then tells Matelda
to lead him to drink of Eunoe, and Matelda obeys "as a
gentle spirit that makes no excuse but makes its will of another's will as soon as it is disclosed by a sign." Matelda
has led Dante through the whole *Paradiso Terrestre*, and
her immediate and joyful obedience to its beauties is the
best symbol of his action. Here again he moves obediently
with her to the stream that will make him ready to leave
the *Paradiso Terrestre* behind and "mount to the stars." At
the same time, as author of the poem, he obeys "the curb of
art" and ceases to write. Dante the pilgrim and Dante the
author, obeying respectively the requirements of that situation in the poem, and the requirements of its writing, coincide as the *Paradiso Terrestre* comes to its end:

> ma perché piene son tutte le carte
> ordite a questa cantica seconda,
> non mi lascia più ir lo fren de l'arte.   (33.139–141)

(But since all the sheets prepared for this second cantica
are full the curb of art does not let me go farther.)

The last four lines return us to Dante the pilgrim, in preparation for the *Paradiso:*

> Io ritornai dalla santissima onda
> rifatto sì come piante novelle
> rinovellate di novella fronda,
> puro e disposto a salire a le stelle.

(From the most holy waters I came forth again remade,
even as new plants renewed with new leaves, pure and
ready to mount to the stars.)

When he has reached the heavens he will see the truth of
much that appeared to him only in visual figures here below.
But the *Paradiso Terrestre* is presented only as it could
appear to Dante the man, and be recorded by Dante the
poet.

In *The Tempest* Prospero proceeds in act 5 to dismount
the make-believe he had set up to make his play. First he
renounces the power of his poetry, which had created the
beauties and the storms of nature, and wakened the sleepers
in their graves; and he breaks his staff and drowns his book.
He then summons the castaways and releases them from
the spells that had held them on the island:

> Their understanding
> Begins to swell, and the approaching tide
> Will shortly fill the reasonable shores
> That now lie foul and muddy.   (5.1)

He removes his magician's gown, and with Ariel's aid he
appears dressed as the Duke of Milan. As the castaways
begin to realize that they are safe after all he shows them
Ferdinand alive and well, playing chess with Miranda. And
when Ariel has brought the master and the boatswain, and
then Caliban, Stephano, and Trinculo, he can at last re-
lease that sprite, the embodiment of his imagination: "Then
to the elements / Be free, and fare you well." That leaves
Prospero, not as the poet or the magician, or even the duke
of Milan, but as the player-author who had made believe
everything, and having ended it all, is now completely
dependent on the good will of his audience:

> Now my charms are all o'erthrown,
> And what strength I have's mine own,
> Which is most faint. (Epilogue)

He begs for their applause:

> Let me not
> Since I have my dukedom got,
> And pardoned the deceiver, dwell
> In this bare island by your spell,
> But release me from my bands
> With the help of your good hands.

He is only a sinner like his audience:

> Now I want
> Spirits to enforce, art to enchant;
> And my ending is despair,
> Unless I be relieved by prayer,
> Which pierces so that it assaults
> Mercy itself, and frees all faults.
> As you from crimes would pardoned be,
> Let your indulgence set me free.

The moment corresponds to the end of Dante's canto 33, when the motives of the fiction and the fictioneer run out, and the protagonist and the poet are deflated into one, a helpless man among men.

In the two works that I have been discussing it is evident, I think, that the art of each poet was consciously fed by many analogies to religion. As the saint must believe the extrarational word of God in order to understand, so the reader must make-believe the poet's fiction in order to get *its* meaning. Poetry, like the Bible, presents evidence of things not seen. But in poetry the unseen thing is not God but action, or love, the ceaseless movement of the human spirit.

Notes

Chapter I

1. E. M. W. Tillyard, *Shakespeare's History Plays* (London: Chatto and Windus, 1956).

2. Erich Auerbach, *Mimesis: The Representation of Reality in Western Literature*, trans. Willard R. Trask (Princeton: Princeton University Press, 1953), and *Scenes from the Drama of European Literature: Six Essays* (New York: Meridian Books, 1959).

3. T. S. Eliot, *Selected Essays*, new ed. (New York: Harcourt, Brace, 1950), p. 225.

4. Shakespeare, *Hamlet*, Laurel Shakespeare (New York: Dell, 1958). All quotations from Shakespeare are taken from the Laurel edition, edited by Francis Fergusson.

5. Dante, Letter 10, *Latin Works*, trans. A. C. Ferrers Howell, Temple Classics (London: Dent, 1929).

6. Aristotle, *Poetics*, trans. S. H. Butcher (New York: Hill and Wang, 1961), p. 62.

7. *De Monarchia*, trans. Philip H. Wicksteed, *Latin Works*.

8. The Italian text of *The Divine Comedy* is drawn from Charles S. Singleton's bilingual edition, Bollingen Series 80 (Princeton: Princeton University Press, 1975). The translation of the passage, 11. 103–131 passim, from *Paradiso*, part 1, is by John D. Sinclair.

9. *Summa Theologica*, I, 1, 10 ad. 1, in *Commentary on St. Paul's Epistle to the Ephesians*, trans. Matthew L. Lamb (Albany, N.Y.: Magi Books, 1966), p. 15.

10. Quoted in J. W. Blench, *Preaching in England in the Late Fifteenth and Sixteenth Centuries: A Study of English Sermons* (New York: Barnes & Noble, 1964), p. 57.

11. C. S. Lewis, *The Allegory of Love: A Study in Medieval Tradition* (London: Oxford University Press, 1936).

Chapter II

1. Ezra Pound, *The Spirit of Romance* (London: Dutton, 1910).

2. Dante, *Convivio*, trans. Philip H. Wicksteed, Temple Classics (London: Dent, 1924), pp. 64, 65.

3. Dante, *Vita Nuova and Canzoniere of Dante Alighieri*, trans. Thomas Okey, Temple Classics (London: Dent, 1948).

4. Geoffrey Bullough, ed., *Narrative and Dramatic Sources of Shakespeare*, vol. 1 (New York: Columbia University Press, 1957).

5. Aristotle, *The Nicomachean Ethics*, trans. H. Rackhem, Loeb Classics Library (London: Heineman, 1934).

6. Denis de Rougemont, *Love in the Western World*, trans. Montgomery Belgion, rev. ed. (New York: Pantheon, 1954).

Chapter IV

1. Geoffrey Bullough, ed., *Narrative and Dramatic Sources of Shakespeare*, vol. 2 (New York: Columbia University Press, 1958).

Chapter VII

1. Mark Van Doren, *Shakespeare* (New York: Holt, 1939), p. 323.

2. The quotations from *The Waste Land* and *Marina* are taken from T. S. Eliot, *The Complete Poems and Plays 1909–1950* (New York: Harcourt, Brace, 1952).

Index

PR   Fergusson, Francis.
2976
F42   Trope and allegory

DATE		
JUN 1 '86		
DEC 1 '86		
FEB 17 '92		
MAY 18 '92		
FEB 07 '94		
MAR 07 '94		

45C63